AF247490

"This book on DAOs is written by two authorities in the field. It is especially pertinent for individuals in financial services seeking to understand the radical differences between DAOs and traditional hierarchical business models, and the opportunities and risks they entail."

Stephen Barnham
Global Chief Digital and Information Officer,
Dai-ichi Life Holdings

"To Dao or not to Dao? This deep dive will answer your questions on what are DAOs and why they matter for the future of finance!"

Ronit Ghose
Global Head, Future of Finance, Citi

"This book is a great combination of scientifically derived research, practical comments, and anecdotes from the blockchain industry. Especially in the second chapter 'Blockchains: The Operating Systems of DAOs', the authors elaborate on the functionalities of a blockchain and its limitations such as the Blockchain Trilemma and explain why the blockchain can and has to be considered as the backbone of a DAO. The entire book is a great read for practitioners, researchers, and also people who want to get started with the topic."

Dr Bernhard Kronfellner
Partner & AD at the Boston Consulting Group

Decentralized Autonomous Organizations

How Finance can Interact with Blockchain-based DAOs

Singapore University of Social Sciences - World Scientific Future Economy Series

ISSN: 2661-3905

Series Editor
David Lee Kuo Chuen *(Singapore University of Social Sciences, Singapore)*

Subject Editors
Guan Chong *(Singapore University of Social Sciences, Singapore)*
Ding Ding *(Singapore University of Social Sciences, Singapore)*

Singapore University of Social Sciences - World Scientific Future Economy Series introduces the new technology trends and challenges that businesses today face, financial management in the digital economy, blockchain technology, smart contract and cryptography. The authors describe current issues that the business leaders and finance professionals are facing, as well as developments in digitalisation. The series covers several increasingly important new areas such as the fourth industrial revolution, Internet of Things (IoT), blockchain technology, artificial intelligence (AI) and many other forces of disruption and breakthroughs that shape today's realities of the economy. A better understanding of the changing environment in the future economy can enable business professionals and leaders to recognise realities, embrace changes, and create new opportunities — locally and globally — in this inevitable digital age.

*Published**

Vol. 9   *Decentralized Autonomous Organizations:*
How Finance can Interact with Blockchain-based DAOs
by Daniel Liebau and Sandy Oh

Vol. 8   *Global Web3 Eco Innovation*
by DeFiDAO, David Lee Kuo Chuen, Guan Chong and Ding Ding

Vol. 7   *Inclusive Disruption: Digital Capitalism, Deep Technology and*
Trade Disputes
by David Lee Kuo Chuen, Linda Low, Joseph Lim and
Carmen Shih Chia Mei

Vol. 6   *Financial Management in the Digital Economy*
edited by David Lee Kuo Chuen, Ding Ding and Guan Chong

Vol. 5   *The Digital Transformation of Property in Greater China: Finance, 5G,*
AI, and Blockchain
by Paul Schulte, Dean Sun and Roman Shemakov

**More information on this series can also be found at*
https://www.worldscientific.com/series/susswsfes

(Continued at end of book)

Singapore University of Social Sciences – World Scientific Future Economy Series **9**

Decentralized Autonomous Organizations

How Finance can Interact with Blockchain-based DAOs

Daniel Liebau
Sandy Oh
Singapore Management University, Singapore

Published by

World Scientific Publishing Co. Pte. Ltd.

5 Toh Tuck Link, Singapore 596224

USA office: 27 Warren Street, Suite 401-402, Hackensack, NJ 07601

UK office: 57 Shelton Street, Covent Garden, London WC2H 9HE

Library of Congress Cataloging-in-Publication Data
Names: Liebau, Daniel, author. | Oh, Sandy, author.
Title: Decentralized autonomous organizations : how finance can interact with blockchain-based
    DAOs / Daniel Liebau, Sandy Oh, Singapore Management University, Singapore.
Description: Singapore ; Hackensack, NJ : World Scientific, [2025] |
    Series: Singapore University of Social Sciences--World Scientific future economy series,
    2661-3905 ; vol. 9 | Includes bibliographical references and index.
Identifiers: LCCN 2024031927 | ISBN 9789811295782 (hardcover) |
    ISBN 9789811295799 (ebook) | ISBN 9789811295805 (ebook other)
Subjects: LCSH: Finance--Technological innovations. | Decentralized autonomous organizations.
Classification: LCC HG173 .L53 2025 | DDC 332--dc23/eng/20240719
LC record available at https://lccn.loc.gov/2024031927

British Library Cataloguing-in-Publication Data
A catalogue record for this book is available from the British Library.

For any available supplementary material, please visit
https://www.worldscientific.com/worldscibooks/10.1142/13918#t=suppl

Desk Editors: Kannan Krishnan/Yulin Jiang

Typeset by Stallion Press
Email: enquiries@stallionpress.com

Disclaimer

The use of general descriptive names, registered names, trademarks, service marks, etc. in this publication does not imply, even in the absence of a specific statement, that such names are exempt from the relevant protective laws and regulations and therefore free for general use.

The publisher, the authors, and the editors are safe to assume that the advice and information in this book are believed to be true and accurate at the date of publication. Neither the publisher nor the authors or the editors give a warranty, expressed or implied, with respect to the material contained herein or for any errors or omissions that may have been made.

The advice and strategies contained herein may not be suitable for your situation. You should consult with a professional where appropriate. Neither the publisher nor the editors or the authors shall be liable for any loss of profit or any other commercial damages, including but not limited to special, incidental, consequential, or other damages.

Foreword

"We need to be more like Facebook, we need to move fast and break things, we need to fail fast and often" — those comments used to send shivers down my spine. As the Group Chief Operating Officer of a large global bank, in one of the most heavily regulated industries, I found the mantra of "fail fast and fail often" deeply unsettling when applied to our approach to innovation.

The banking sector, scarred by the global financial crisis under intense regulatory scrutiny, operates in a vastly different realm from the tech startups that popularized this philosophy. In our world, failure isn't just a learning opportunity — it can have far-reaching consequences that ripple through the global economy.

Post financial crisis, regulators have tightened their grip, demanding not just compliance but accountability. They want to see tangible consequences for failure and a clear line of responsibility. This shift has created a palpable tension within the industry.

How can we foster innovation when the stakes for failure are so high? Imagine trying to encourage your team to think outside the box when a misstep could potentially end careers or trigger regulatory backlash. It is like asking someone to perform a high-wire act without a safety net — in front of a global audience.

This environment poses a significant challenge: How do we create a culture of innovation where staff feel empowered to experiment with new ideas, pilot cutting-edge technologies, and create value for our company and clients, all while navigating the minefield of regulatory compliance? It is a delicate balancing act that requires a complete reimagining of how we approach risk and innovation in the financial services sector.

Enter Daniel Liebau and Sandy Oh's groundbreaking work on *Decentralized Autonomous Organizations (DAOs): How Finance can Interact with Blockchain-based DAOs.* Their work is like a breath of fresh air in a stagnant room.

Daniel and Sandy have over 30 years of combined experience in financial services, spanning sales, operations, technology, and governance. Their expertise covers traditional finance and blockchain, positioning them uniquely to address the questions about DAOs in the industry. As practitioners, researchers, and educators, they bridge the knowledge gap between blockchain technology and traditional financial markets. Their book is a culmination of this experience and expertise.

Instead of merely commending the virtues of DAOs or painting a utopian picture of decentralized finance, they offer something far more valuable: a thoughtful, measured path for responsible engagement and experimentation within the financial services sector.

A significant portion of their work is dedicated to risk management — music to the ears of any banking executive. They don't shy away from the challenges; instead, they confront them head-on, offering potential approaches for financial services companies to not only get comfortable with the risks but also become genuinely curious about the opportunities DAOs present.

Their work serves as a roadmap for how traditional financial institutions can dip their toes into the waters of decentralized finance without diving headfirst into regulatory hot water. It is about finding that sweet spot between innovation and compliance, between embracing new technologies and maintaining the stability that the global financial system demands.

What makes this perspective so exciting is its potential to bridge the gap between the old and the new, the centralised and the decentralized. It is not about replacing traditional banking but about evolving it to meet the needs of a rapidly changing digital landscape.

DAOs represent more than just a technological innovation; they are an entirely new client segment with unique needs and opportunities. For financial institutions willing to adapt, this could open up unprecedented avenues for growth and innovation.

The book isn't just theoretical musing — it's a practical guide for those of us in the financial services sector who want to leverage the opportunities presented by this new paradigm responsibly. It's about staying relevant in a world where the very concept of money and financial services is being redefined.

As we stand at the crossroads of traditional finance and the decentralized future, works like this are invaluable. They remind us that innovation doesn't have to mean recklessness and that even in the most regulated industries, there is room for transformative change — if approached with wisdom, foresight, and a deep understanding of both the risks and the rewards. For anyone in the financial service industry looking to navigate the exciting yet treacherous waters of decentralized finance, this isn't just recommended reading — it's essential. It's time to move beyond the fear of failure and embrace a new era of responsible innovation in finance.

About Doris Honold

Doris Honold is an accomplished strategic leader with over 25 years of C-Suite and board-level experience in Finance, Risk, and Change Management. Her extensive career in global banking has included senior positions, such as Chief Risk Officer of Market Risk and Group, and Chief Operating Officer (COO) at major institutions like Standard Chartered Bank. Honold's international experience spans Germany, Japan, Singapore, and the UK, providing her with a comprehensive understanding of global financial markets and regulatory environments. Honold currently serves on the board of several financial services companies, leveraging her deep understanding of risk management in both traditional and digital banking environments.

Preface

In true digital style, we first met online. It was 2020, the year of COVID-19. Dan taught an online course on blockchain and digital assets at Singapore Management University, and Sandy was a participant. That sowed the seeds for our friendship and collaboration in education and writing. We discovered many similarities between us, including early careers in banking, followed by a transition to the world of entrepreneurship and digital assets. Our shared optimism for the transformative potential of open blockchain technology and DAOs is the catalyst for this book.

Although DAOs have not hit the mainstream yet, they have potential as a new form of organization for global decentralized collaboration and digital governance. Where only individuals initially used DAOs to organize and pursue common interests, now countries and supranational bodies are paying attention to them too.[1,2] As we write this in May of 2024, innovative leaders in the financial services industry are already interacting with DAOs. While there are books that introduce readers to a general understanding of DAOs,

---

[1] https://www.acnnewswire.com/press-release/english/88247/united-nations-igf-dynamic-coalition-pilots-a-decentralized-autonomous-organization-(dao) (accessed on 21 May 2024).
[2] https://www.ecb.europa.eu/pub/pdf/scpops/ecb.op331~a03e416045.en.pdf (accessed on 3 June 2024).

as far as we know, there is no book specifically for financial service professionals to comprehend DAOs in detail and assess their idiosyncratic risks. Our book addresses this gap.

With a combined experience of over 30 years in various parts of financial services, including investments, sales, operations, governance, and technology, we understand the industry's constraints and regulatory obligations. Our more recent experience in digital assets, another 15 years combined, allows us to comprehend the potential that DAOs may hold. The book's target audience spans the financial services industry, from banks and brokerages to custodians, insurers, asset managers, payment service providers, and exchanges. The book is particularly relevant for those involved in client onboarding decisions and Know Your Client (KYC) roles, as well as senior management making strategic decisions. While we are not legal experts, we understand the importance of legal and regulatory risks in this context and have included sections to address them. This book also serves as a valuable resource for entrepreneurs, academics, researchers, and students.

As realist optimists, our natural inclination is to be balanced and grounded. Unbridled techno-optimism, the norm in the crypto universe, is not our style. Our critical attitude influences how we research, debate and present our findings. Where possible and relevant, we reference peer-reviewed research and present both the opportunities and risks of financial services entities interacting with DAOs as novel clients or service providers. Notwithstanding our sober approach, we aim to stimulate your intellectual curiosity with the potentialities of DAOs and provide you with a comprehensive, no-hype guide to navigate this new frontier. We hope this book not only assists those in the financial services and blockchain industries but also contributes to global regulatory and policy-level discussions and preparation on DAO engagement.

We look forward to hearing your views and feedback. Email us at info@lightbulbcap.com.

About the Authors

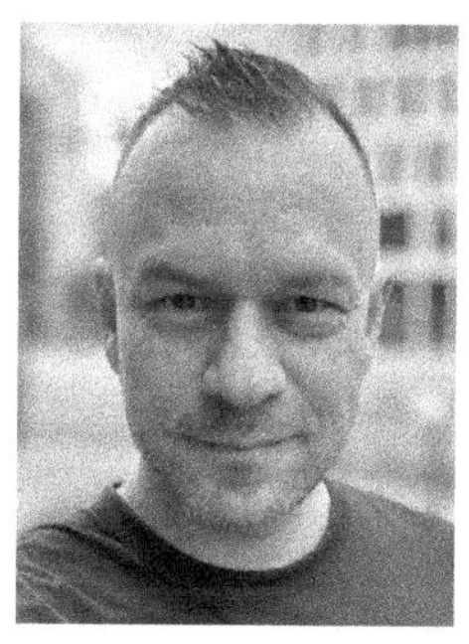 **Daniel Liebau** (Dan) is a pracademic: As a practitioner, he is the Founder of Lightbulb Capital in Hong Kong and Singapore. Previously, Dan was the CIO of the Modular Blockchain Fund at Modular Asset Management and the COO of HSBC Securities in Singapore. As an academic, he is an Affiliate Faculty Member at Singapore Management University where he teaches courses on Cryptography, Blockchain and Digital Assets, and Decentralized Finance (DeFi). Previously, he was a Visiting Professor at IE Business School, where he received the teaching excellence award. His research work investigates blockchain in the financial markets context and has been published in various academic journals by Springer and MIT Press. He is also the Associate Editor-in-Chief of World Scientific's *Annual Review of Fintech* journal. Dan is completing his PhD in Finance at Erasmus University in 2024 and holds Master's degrees in Innovation (SMU) and Finance (IE).

Sandy Oh is an ardent believer in the power of lifelong learning and education. She is an Associate Instructor and Advisor to Lightbulb Capital, a Singapore and Hong Kong-based firm that collaborates with members of the financial industry to learn and adopt transformational technology. She is also the Co-Founder of Nomadism, a Circular Design consultancy. Through Singapore Management University's Academy, Sandy teaches classes on blockchain, digital assets and non-fungible tokens (NFTs). Prior to discovering blockchain and its myriad applications, Sandy held senior fixed income sales roles in HSBC, Jefferies, ING, Commerzbank, and J.P. Morgan. She has an MBA from the University of Chicago Booth School of Business and a BA in Politics, Philosophy and Economics from Oxford University.

Acknowledgments

David Lee: David, without you, this book would not exist. Thank you for introducing Daniel to the exciting blockchain world, agreeing to add our book to your FinTech series at World Scientific, and being a kind guide in an ambiguous world.

Kenneth Bok: Ken, we benefited from your authorly experience in the nitty gritty of how to get a book written and published. Thank you for sharing so generously.

Michael Gilmore: Michael, your advice was invaluable. You guided us first-time authors on how to choose and work with a publisher and how to market our book.

Vanessa Ward: Vanessa, thank you for your manifold support — from guiding us on how we should think about our book cover to patiently designing it for us. Your cakes and cookies, baked with love, gave us sustenance in working toward the book's deadline.

Yulin Jiang: Yulin, thank you for supporting us as the editor of our book. Your assistance was strategically important. We appreciate you onboarding us as new authors and for being available and supportive throughout.

ChatGTP and Claude.ai and Grammarly.com: We never used any of your outputs uncritically in our book. We always carefully reviewed your suggestions. Regardless, you deserve a mention here and we thank you for your support during ideation.

Contents

PART 1

Chapter 1

Origin, Purpose, Definitions, and Opportunities of DAOs

Abstract

Decentralized autonomous organizations (DAOs) represent a novel form of human coordination enabled by blockchain technology. This chapter explores the historical context and theoretical underpinnings of DAOs, drawing on concepts from organizational theory, game theory, and the study of public goods. It examines how DAOs aim to address traditional agency problems in corporate governance by aligning the interests of principals and agents through decentralized decision-making and transparency. The chapter traces the controversial history of the first well-known DAO called "the DAO" and ends with a discussion on the growing relevance of DAOs in the financial services industry as potential clients, investment opportunities, and service providers to established institutions.

1.1 Introduction and opportunities

"Fiction isn't bad. It is vital. Without commonly accepted stories about things like money, states, or corporations, no complex human society can function," says Harari (2015) in *Homo Deus*. Fiction is simply shared narratives created by human societies. In fact, it is the ability of humans to create and believe in shared stories that differentiate us from animals and enable us to evolve and form complex cultures, social structures, and institutions. Furthermore, technology interacts with our narratives, potentially leading to new forms of storytelling and belief systems.

Money is a fitting illustration of this idea. When Satoshi Nakamoto created bitcoin (BTC) in 2009, one BTC was worth nothing. Satoshi inscribed the words *"The Times* 03/Jan/2009 Chancellor on brink of second bailout for banks" on BTC's genesis block, possibly as a provocative criticism of the failure of central banking during the Great Financial Crisis. No one at that time, not even Satoshi, could have predicted that 14 years later, BTC ETFs would be issued by the largest fund manager in the world, Blackrock, approved by financial services regulators and embraced by some of the most astute hedge fund managers like Millennium, Point72, and Elliot.[1]

What about corporations? Harari argues that they are legal fictions created by humans to enable large-scale cooperation and economic activity. Seen in this light, could DAOs be an evolution of humans using new blockchain technology to cooperate and organize? The very first DAO (known as "the DAO") was launched in 2006 on the Ethereum network. "The DAO" was a spectacular failure, and DAOs could have been completely written off. However, fast forward to May 2024, Securitize Markets, a distributor of Blackrock's first tokenized fund BUIDL, applied to become Arbitrum DAO's service provider in assisting with the diversification of its highly concentrated treasury portfolio. These examples show that new technology adoption and organizational evolution are neither predictable nor linear. Rather, they have been and will continue to be erratic, volatile, and controversial. It is with sensitivity against this backdrop that we present the development of DAOs and how financial services professionals should learn to interact with them.

This book has three parts and eight chapters. In Part 1, we lay the foundations for understanding DAOs. Chapter 1 traces the origin and definitions of DAOs. We situate DAOs' purpose and relevance in the context of the historical development of human coordination and organization. The chapter addresses why DAOs matter for financial services professionals. Chapter 2 explains the technical characteristics

---

[1] https://www.bloomberg.com/news/articles/2024-05-16/millennium-point72-and-citadel-are-among-buyers-of-bitcoin-etfs (accessed on 22 May 2024).

of blockchains so that readers can assess the capabilities and limitations of DAOs built on these platforms. Since DAOs represent such a fundamental shift in how governance is carried out, we dedicate Chapter 3 to DAO governance and dispute resolution. We review how the new technology has enabled the ability to carry out new ways of governance and voting. DAO governance processes differ significantly from traditional organizations, and readers must comprehend these differences to effectively evaluate DAOs.

In Part 2, we present our approach to deciphering the different types of DAOs and assess their risks in a structured way. Chapter 4 introduces our framework of categorizing DAOs along objectives, community, governance, economics, finance, technology, and legal and regulatory aspects. This framework acts as a checklist of DAO features that the reader can use to understand DAOs' objectives and characteristics. Chapter 5 defines the idiosyncratic risks DAOs pose. We define accountability risk, community risk, financial risk, governance risk, and operational and technology risks specifically within the DAO context. Our DAO risk assessment methodology is crucial for financial services professionals in assessing risks for the emerging organizational form and in considering how to interact with DAOs as future clients or service providers. In Chapter 6, we show how to use our methodology in analyzing two case studies: MakerDAO and KlimaDAO.

Part 3 contains interviews with industry and key takeaways and challenges for DAO adoption. Chapter 7 features four interviews with a diversity of ecosystem participants. Hagen Rooke, a partner at the law firm Reed Smith, provides valuable insights into the legal implications and challenges surrounding the formation and operation of DAOs from the perspective of a seasoned legal professional working at the intersection of law, financial regulation, and emerging technologies. Sharon Lourdes Paul, Co-Founder and CEO of HQ.xyz, talks about how her company helps DAOs bridge the gap between traditional and decentralized financial systems, including their platform for managing DAO treasury flows and accounting. Dr. Sinclair Davidson, a Professor at the Royal Melbourne Institute of Technology (RMIT) and Co-Founder of the University's Blockchain

Hub, applies existing economic theories to present DAOs as hybrid organizational forms that combine the aspects of markets, firms, and government, and provides an update on the status of DAO research. Bill Laboon, Director of Education and Governance Initiatives at Web3 Foundation, discusses his experience in growing the Polkadot ecosystem and his role in the Polkadot DAO.

In our last chapter, we review the key takeaways and challenges for DAO adoption. This is also where we allow our imagination to roam and expand on more speculative uses of DAOs before ending on the note of how the finance industry should position itself. Our hope is by the end of this book, the reader will have the knowledge and insights necessary to address the question "To DAO, or not to DAO?"

1.2   Context for the emergence of DAOs

To situate the significance of DAOs, we first ask the following questions: How do human societies organize themselves? How do these organizations interact with each other and how do they collectively impact the wider world? Throughout history, we have formed tribes, institutions, and networks (Ronfeldt, 1996). One way of comparing these forms of organizational structures is to differentiate them between hierarchies and networks. In a hierarchy, there is a clear chain of command from the top to the bottom. Each person in a hierarchy has a clear role in the organization, and their power and responsibility are dictated by their position. Networks refer to a form of organization based on connections between individuals and groups of entities. Compared to a hierarchy, these relationships are more emergent and fluid, and less formal (Fig. 1.1).

In a hierarchy, decisions are made quickly and efficiently. The leader gives the command, and the rest follow. Clearly, when the situation is chaotic and requires speed of action, a hierarchy is able to respond swiftly. However, "information at the edge" (Calcaterra and Kaal, 2020) is unable to flow effectively from the bottom of the organization to the higher rungs, which can mean the leaders at the

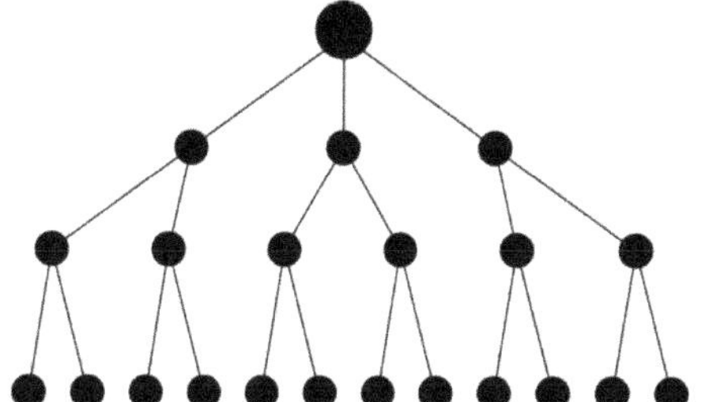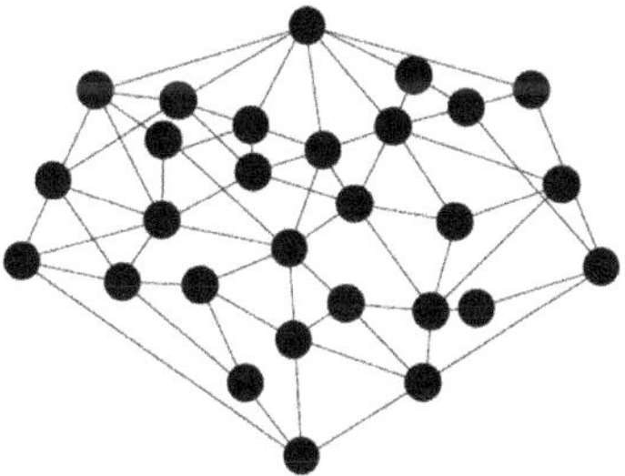

Fig. 1.1. Hierarchy vs. network. On the left is the hierarchy with its distinct levels of seniority, and on the right is the network with its decentralized, flat structure of interconnected nodes.

top make decisions with incomplete information. The centralization of power brings other challenges too. Over time, if hierarchies stay stagnant and ossify, they become inflexible and unable to deal with new competition and crisis. Also, if there are no checks and balances on hierarchical leadership, there is always the corrupting temptation of power.

In contrast, decentralized networks have no single dominant source of authority. Instead, a network contains multiple nodes that communicate and interact with each other directly. Failure of certain nodes does not take the whole system down, making the overall system more resilient. Without a strict hierarchy, individuals have more freedom and independence for action. Information flows more freely among all points in the network. Such diverse flows could produce better results from the wisdom of the crowd. In the famous experiment by Galton in 1907, hundreds of participants at a fair guessed the weight of an ox. The crowd's median guess was remarkably accurate even though the individual guesses were far off.

In *The Square and the Tower*, Ferguson (2017) observes that historical accounts tend to overweigh the importance of hierarchies in shaping history. He challenges this dominant view by showing how networks operating from the Reformation to the current internet and social media times are equally important. Networks have the power to disrupt established hierarchies and create significant changes in societies. DAOs operate as networks, and their potential for disruption should be recognized.

Of course, the wisdom of the crowd could easily turn into the folly of the masses if certain conditions are not present. The network could be populated by individuals with no expertise, or diversity, or independence of thought (Surowiecki, 2005). The current scourge of disinformation demonstrates the dangers of powerful negative network effects. Lastly, herding a decentralized network is energetically more intensive.

Besides hierarchy versus network, organizational theorists use other frameworks to compare organizational development. In *Reinventing Organizations*, Laloux (2014) analyzes different organizational paradigms by highlighting their distinct characteristics, values, and objectives. In his classification, Amber Organizations are seen in traditional bureaucracies where rules and processes dominate, for example, the army. Orange Organizations are focused on performance and profit, and most for-profit companies would fit into this category. As organizations look beyond the profit motive to social responsibility, sustainability, and ethical practices, they become Green Organizations. In Laloux's framework, Teal Organizations are the ones that allow for most individual autonomy. They operate on the principles of self-organization where decision-making is distributed among people based on knowledge and expertise rather than hierarchy. To employ the use of metaphors to explain this shift, the organization may move from being a machine to an organism within a larger complex system (Morgan, 1986). As part of a system, organizations must consider their impact on other parties and stakeholders. Consensus is reached via other creative ways rather than simply deferring to authority. In the process, members feel empowered and experience a greater sense of fulfillment and purpose. As we shall see in later sections, the structure of DAOs can enable this paradigm shift. DAO membership tends to be self-selecting as individuals voluntarily join DAOs whose causes resonate with theirs. After joining, their motivation and incentives influence the degree of engagement. Through token ownership, members are also often owners of DAOs, which potentially leads to more skin in the game.

1.2.1 *Public goods, game theory, and coordination*

The world faces an urgent and critical challenge in the effective coordination and governance of public goods. From the rapid depletion of our planet's rainforests to the growing scarcity of clean water resources, the consequences of mismanagement and lack of coordination in public goods are devastating. To understand the growing relevance of DAOs, this section will start with introducing the theoretical underpinnings of public goods, followed by an explanation of coordination failure in the governing of public goods and the solutions addressing the failure.

The most common definition of public goods in economics textbooks is that they are non-excludable and non-rivalrous. Excludability refers to the degree to which users can access a good, service, or resource. For example, consumer products like mobile phones are in this category. Apple can restrict purchases to only paying customers and exclude non-paying customers. If a good is non-excludable, it is costly or almost impossible to exclude another person from using the good. For example, when a country provides national defense, it must protect everyone within its borders. The country is unable to limit its national defense to specific citizens. Rivalry means one person's use or consumption of the product reduces or prevents another person from using it. Using the example of national defense, one citizen's "consumption" of it does not reduce or prevent another citizen from enjoying the benefit, making it non-rivalrous. In contrast, with mobile phones, one customer's purchase of a phone prevents another person from buying it.

The concepts of excludability and rivalry are attributed to economists Paul Samuelson (1954) and Richard Musgrave (Desmarais-Tremblay, 2017). Although these economists introduced the theory of excludability and rivalry, in practice, goods and services are not always so clearly delineated. Exclusion and rivalry exist in degrees for goods and resources. As Ver Eecke (1999) argues, public goods are a valid but "ideal concept." Let us use some examples to illustrate this point. Are libraries public or private goods? Many public libraries require you to prove you are living in that state to be a member. Based on this criterion, libraries have a degree of excludability. Are they rivalrous? Ariel's membership of the library does not prevent Bobbi from joining, so libraries are non-rivalrous. Hence, public libraries are a type of public goods where the cost of exclusion is low.

It is important to remember that the theories of exclusion and rivalry were introduced before the dominance of digital technology. Now, how can we classify digital goods on the public spectrum? If we use the characteristics of non-exclusion and non-rivalry, one example of public goods is Wikipedia. More recently, The Digital Public Goods Alliance (DPGA), a United Nations-endorsed body, defines public digital goods as "open source software, open data, open AI systems, and open content collections that adhere to privacy, and other applicable laws and best practices."[2] One example of DPGA digital public goods is Fedora Linux.

Next, we delve into understanding how organizations make decisions. Organizations are continuously weighing and selecting among different options and courses of action. To understand how they make decisions, game theory is often used. Game theory is a relatively new field of study developed by mathematician John von Neumann and economist Oskar Morgenstern (1944). It uses models to study the strategic interaction between game players in times of cooperation and conflict, and has been widely used in diverse fields, including the study of firms, markets, and nation states. One of the most cited games is the Prisoners' Dilemma. In this game, two people (let's call them Ariel and Bobbi) are arrested for a crime. They are interrogated separately and must decide whether to confess or keep silent. If Ariel keeps silent, and Bobbi confesses, Ariel goes to jail and Bobbi goes free. Ariel reasons that it is better to confess. Bobbi goes through the same reasoning and confesses too. Both confess, which is a worse outcome than if both had coordinated beforehand to stay silent. This is a classic example of a coordination failure and has been used in many ways to illustrate how the pursuit of self-interest has led to the detriment of group interest.

---

[2]https://digitalpublicgoods.net/digital-public-goods (accessed on 5 October 2023).

The idea behind the Prisoners' Dilemma was first conceived by Dreshner and Flood (1950) as part of RAND Corporation's study of global nuclear strategy.[3] In their setup, the two players are the US and the Soviet Union. Each country must decide whether to spend its budget on nuclear weapons or not. If they decide not to, they help reduce the risk of a nuclear accident and have more budget for other important fiscal expenditure items. If they don't spend on nuclear, and the other country does, their competitor becomes more powerful geopolitically. Based on this reasoning, both countries end up spending on nuclear weapons. This deterrence explains the current conundrum where nation states refuse to give up nuclear arms despite the existential threat of nuclear war.

In game theory, a coordination failure occurs when the players are unable to arrive at a mutually beneficial outcome due to a breakdown in working together. Although various outcomes are possible, the players fail to choose the optimal result due to a lack of trust, communication, common knowledge, or credible commitment. Coordination failures are the root causes of a lot of issues in society and relationships, including "Tragedy of the Commons."

The "Tragedy of the Commons" arises when a public good is depleted by the self-interested action of individuals. In the short term, the individual benefits at the expense of others. But in the long term, everyone is worse off. The term was coined by Hardin (1968) and has since been used to understand many collective action problems, such as overfishing, deforestation, pollution, overgrazing, and congestion. Such problems are also known as negative externalities, which are costs or harm to a third party that is not accounted for by the party that generated the cost.

How do we deal with such coordination failures? For one, we have come to rely on formal rules and regulations. These could be set and imposed by governments or private bodies. Rules and regulations remove ambiguity and set common expectations and standards. This helps to give a sense of fairness and confidence. Fees and

---

[3]https://plato.stanford.edu/Archives/Win2004/entries/prisoner-dilemma (accessed on 11 July 2023).

penalties are imposed on those who create negative externalities. For example, fishing quotas are used to cap and control overfishing. Nuclear arms control treaties are used to limit, regulate, or reduce the development of nuclear weapons. However, rules and regulations are not sufficient. We only need to turn to the news to be reminded daily of the destruction of valuable natural resources and the existential threats of climate change.

In contrast, Nobel Prize winner Elinor Ostrom shows in *Governing the Commons* (1990) that government regulation and privatization are not necessarily the only or best way to protect public goods. In Ostrom's field studies of small local communities, she discovered that it is possible for a group of individuals to work together to address shared problems and manage common resources successfully. Also known as collective action, this involves people coming together voluntarily to create and enforce their own rules and norms to guide their interactions and responsibilities. In many ways, Elinor Ostrom's eight design principles for successful collective action form the philosophical underpinnings of DAOs. In fact, some DAO founders pay tribute to her work in their writings, for example, in Moloch DAO. Where Ostrom's case studies are of 50 to 15,000 people in local and low-tech environments, DAOs are for large-scale global communities enabled by blockchains and smart contracts. Given the difference in scale, it remains to be seen whether Ostrom's principles can be fully applied to globally distributed internet-based DAOs with potentially millions of members. At a minimum, the common thread is the belief that there are alternative ways of organization away from a centralized state that can be used to solve coordination problems. One of Ostrom's recommendations is to ensure that rules are relevant to local needs and conditions. Also, those affected by the rules should be able to modify the rules. DAOs facilitate members' participation in decision-making by voting methods, which we will discuss in Chapter 3. Ostrom recommends there should be a system for monitoring behavior and penalties for rule-breakers. The penalties should be proportional to the severity of the offense. In Chapter 3 on DAO governance, we build on our technical knowledge to see how DAOs use smart contracts to design processes and incentives to motivate desired behavior and punish undesirable ones, as well as resolve disputes among their members.

1.3 Definitions, purpose, and history of DAOs

1.3.1 *Definitions of DAOs*

The precursor to the DAO is a concept called decentralized autonomous corporation (DAC), first mentioned by technologist Daniel Larimer. In his description, DACs are a new governance form that uses tokenized shares to pay dividends. De Filippi and Hassan (2021) refer to DAOs as "organizations deployed as smart contracts on top of an existing blockchain network." They further add that a DAO "enables people to coordinate and govern themselves mediated by a set of self-executing rules deployed on a public blockchain, and whose governance is decentralized." In the Ethereum white paper, Founder Vitalik Buterin defines a DAO as a "virtual entity that has a certain set of members which have the right to spend the entity's funds and modify its code (...). This essentially replicates the legal trappings of a traditional company or a nonprofit by using only cryptographic blockchain technology for enforcement."[4] Various definitions of DAOs abound, but when we synthesize from them, the following common characteristics emerge: DAOs enable individuals with common goals to coordinate online. There is no central authority and governance is decentralized. A DAO's smart contracts primarily determine the rules of interaction among its members (De Filippi and Hassan, 2016). DAOs run on public blockchains and hence may inherit some of their properties: permissionlessness, transparency, decentralization, and cryptographic security. Last, members of a DAO are typically registered with a unique blockchain address, and they would have purchased governance tokens linked to their address. These tokens are used to participate in the decision-making process

---

[4]https://ethereum.org/en/whitepaper (accessed on 24 July 2023).

(Ding *et al.*, 2023). Using governance tokens to vote on decisions and having voting outcomes recorded on the blockchain constitute an important feature of DAOs. This makes their governance process transparent and auditable. Therefore, for the purpose of this book, we focus on DAOs that have issued governance tokens.

1.3.2 *How DAOs aim to address agency problems*

Given the structural choices with which we can organize, why would we choose a DAO and not a company? What are the advantages of committing operations and management to smart contracts on a blockchain versus using more traditional setups? One way to find answers to these questions is to examine the long-standing agency problem in corporate governance, and then posit how DAOs can be used to address them.

Agency theory studies conflicts between shareholders (principals) and managers (agents). It was first developed by Coase (1937), Jensen and Meckling (1976), and Fama (1980). An agency problem arises when the goals of the principals and agents are in conflict, and it is costly and difficult for the principal to monitor the agent. When management raises funds from shareholders, the latter want the managers' specialized knowledge to generate returns on their capital. The managers, however, may be motivated by other interests not aligned with the shareholders. Agency problems lead to a variety of issues including expropriation of assets at one extreme to misallocation of funds and managerial job entrenchment on the other. Existing solutions to solve such agency problems use contracts to target behavior, for example, salaries, periodic reporting and hierarchical governance, and output, such as stock options and commissions (Eisenhardt, 1989). In these solutions, monitoring costs are high to ensure the alignment of interests between principals and agents. For a more comprehensive survey of corporate governance problems, please refer to Shleifer and Vishny (1997).

In firms, we have shareholders, a board, executives, and managers. The shareholders and board (as principals) spend significant resources monitoring the executives and managers (as agents).

Business decisions are taken by executives typically in a hierarchical top-down way. In DAOs, these agency costs could be significantly reduced because the roles of principals and agents overlap. Typically, DAOs have no boards and executives to dictate decisions. They have flatter structures and decision-making is more dispersed compared to corporations. DAO members can make proposals for discussion and voting. Different DAOs will have their own proposal and voting eligibility. Usually, it requires DAO members to own the required governance tokens which entitle them to voting. In this setup, DAO members inhabit both the roles of principal and agent, and thus help mitigate the agency conflict.

Additionally, DAOs are more transparent in their decision-making. In firms, many significant decisions can be made away from the prying eyes of the public. For DAOs, important decisions are voted upon, and the voting details and their results are publicly visible. Voting can either occur on-chain, recorded on the blockchain, or off-chain, i.e. not recorded on the blockchain. These two characteristics of DAOs — the overlap between principals and agents and the stronger transparency offered by the public nature of blockchains — help reduce conflict of interest (Bellavitis, 2023).

1.3.3 *History: The DAO on Ethereum*

By now, we have introduced sufficient context and definitions to review the formation of the first well-known DAO. Slightly confusingly, it was called "the DAO" and it was created in 2016 on the Ethereum blockchain. It was a highly publicized and widely anticipated project initiated by Christoph and Simon Jentzsch, who were also co-founders of a German startup called Slock.it. The DAO was set up as an automated investment fund. Its whitepaper describes how, for the first time, participants can "maintain direct real-time control of contributed funds, and governance rules are formalized, automated, and enforced using software."[5] During the

---

[5] https://lawofthelevel.lexblogplatformthree.com/wp-content/uploads/sites/187/2017/07/WhitePaper-1.pdf (accessed on 26 July 2023).

28-day crowdfunding period between 30 April 2016 and 29 May 2016, participants sent the native currency of the Ethereum blockchain, known as Ether or ETH, to the DAO in exchange for DAO tokens.[6] The DAO tokens, in turn, would enable their holders to vote and fund Ethereum-related startup investment opportunities. The crowdfunding raised approximately 12 million ETH (in exchange for approximately 1.15 billion DAO tokens). At that time, the raised amount was valued at around USD 150 million.

In a conventional venture fund, investors would entrust the fund managers with their capital and the latter would decide on how to invest the money. In contrast, the DAO enabled the token holders to vote and control how their funds were to be allocated. This meant that they were both principal and agent.

Despite the excitement, various governance and technical issues were raised (Quinn, 2017). These included a technical bug in the DAO code that would allow an attacker to withdraw funds repeatedly. This vulnerability was not dealt with and on 17 June 2016, an attacker began draining the DAO of its ETH balance.[7] Given the transparent nature of blockchains, the Ethereum community watched these transactions happening in real time with shock and dread. Stopping the attacker required speed. However, the decentralized nature of Ethereum and the DAO meant that no majority consensus could be obtained fast enough to stop the attacker. By 22 June 2016, 3,689,577 ETH (which was 30% of the total amount raised) was drained by the attacker into a subsidiary account. This account was subject to a 28-day holding period governed by the DAO smart contract (Quinn, 2017). While the drained funds sat there, the Ethereum and the DAO community debated furiously on solutions from "soft forks" to "hard forks." In the context of blockchains, a soft fork is an upgrade that is backward compatible with its

---

[6]https://www.sec.gov/files/litigation/investreport/34-81207.pdf (accessed on 26 July 2023).

[7]https://blog.chain.link/reentrancy-attacks-and-the-dao-hack (accessed on 28 July 2023).

previous versions. The new rules introduced through a soft fork do not invalidate the blocks and transactions created under the old rules. In contrast, in a hard fork, the new rules are not backward compatible, meaning that the blocks and transactions created under the old rules are invalid on the new chain. A hard fork leads to a permanent split into two separate blockchains and hence is more disruptive than a soft fork.

The DAO was faced with three options: do nothing and allow the attacker to take possession of the funds after the 28-day holding period; implement a soft fork to freeze the siphoned funds; or implement a hard fork to unwind the attack completely; return all siphoned ETH and reimburse DAO participants (Mehar *et al.*, 2019). There was a vocal minority who believed that the attacker was simply responding to the DAO's code as written. Tampering with the blockchain would go against the idea of immutability that was crucial to its censorship resistance feature. In this do-nothing scenario, the attacker would end up keeping the funds. The second camp believed that human intervention was justified as it was ethically wrong for the attacker to steal the funds. In the end, the second camp won. Key members in the Ethereum community, including its influential founder Vitalik Buterin, voted for a hard fork. After all the fanfare, the DAO was dead, and with it, some ideals of techno-utopianism. The minority who did not agree to the "hard fork" split from the main blockchain and formed "Ethereum Classic" with its native currency ETC. As Quinn (2017) observes, the experimental goals that the DAO originally set out to achieve have yet to be brought to fruition. Since then, many DAO builders have learned from the lessons of the DAO and worked toward creating more resilient and secure organizations (Fig. 1.2).

1.4 Why DAOs matter for financial services professionals

In *The Ascent of Money*, Ferguson (2009) traces the central role finance has played in shaping the course of history. Government bonds were instrumental in the financing and outcomes of wars.

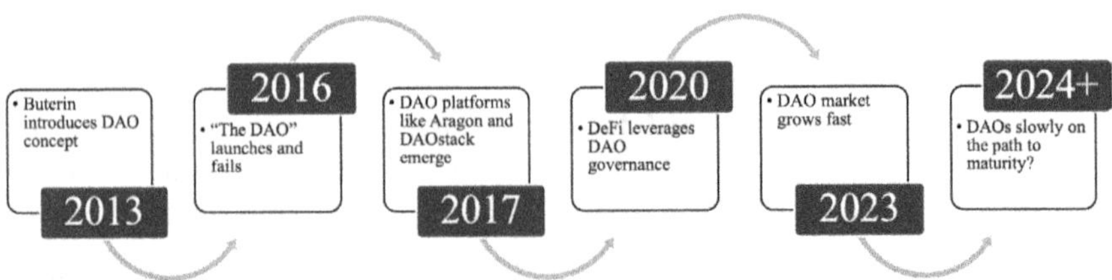

Fig. 1.2. DAO history.

In the 17th century, the creation of the first joint stock company in the Netherlands funded risky sea trading expeditions and expanded commerce. Throughout history, finance allocates resources to entrepreneurial effort and influences the type of activity that gets funded. In turn, this determines the kinds of jobs created and the drivers of growth for the funded entity, be it a firm or a state. The tentacles of finance seep into every facet of our lives, and its effects can be both positive and negative. Finance has the potential to lift living standards or inflict great hardship when bubbles burst or when it deepens inequality. The actions of financial services professionals are intricately linked to the cycles of societal development.

If DAOs are to be a novel and attractive way for individuals to organize, it would then follow that DAOs and financial services would be interacting with each other increasingly. The following example illustrates how a DAO becomes the client of a financial services firm.

Arbitrum is a high-growth technology platform aiming to make the Ethereum blockchain more scalable and affordable. The Arbitrum DAO governs the Arbitrum ecosystem. In May 2024, this DAO controlled approximately USD 4 billion, mostly held in their own cryptocurrency called ARB. The Arbitrum DAO recognizes the concentration risks it is exposed to and hence has initiated the Stable Treasury Endowment Programme (STEP) to diversify its portfolio. Financial intermediaries can apply. The process is similar to an RFP, or request for proposal, a pension fund might issue to allocate some of its capital to a new investment vehicle. Securitize, a tokenization specialist and fund distributor of Blackrock products, has responded to the Arbitrum DAO's request with a proposal to assist with the investment into Blackrock's tokenized BUIDL fund.[8] The fund invests mainly in US treasury bonds and cash. Hence, such an investment product would help the DAO reduce the current high volatility in its portfolio. In June 2024, Arbitrum DAO announced it has decided to invest in six real-world asset (RWA) products, including BUIDL fund.[9]

On the flip side, financial institutions themselves could potentially become clients of DAOs. In the metaverse, there are two popular platforms: The Sandbox and Decentraland. Both Sandbox and Decentraland are governed by their respective DAOs. In 2022 and 2023, several major banks, J.P. Morgan, HSBC, DBS, and Standard Chartered, ventured into the metaverse by purchasing virtual land plots in The Sandbox and Decentraland. These financial institutions, recognizing the potential for growth and opportunities in the virtual world, invested in digital real estate to establish their presence and explore new avenues for customer engagement. By acquiring land in these metaverse platforms, banks aimed to create immersive experiences, showcase their products and services, and tap into the growing interest in virtual economies and digital assets.

As DAOs make innovative use of blockchain technology, they attract builders and entrepreneurs who are experimenting with its potential. As such, DAOs can also be viewed as prospective startup investment opportunities for financial services professionals. For example, venture firm A16z has invested in BreederDAO, CreatorDAO, FingerprintsDAO, and MakerDAO.[10]

Last, can financial services professionals consider using DAOs as an organizational structure themselves? We are seeing forward-thinking lawyers congregate on LexDAO to review best practices and standards for smart contracts to shape the direction of the profession in the digital realm.[11] Scientists and researchers are collaborating

---

[8]https://forum.arbitrum.foundation/t/securitize-markets-buidl-step-application/23652 (accessed on 13 May 2024).

[9]https://thedefiant.io/news/defi/arbitrum-dao-plans-35m-arb-investment-into-on-chain-rwas (accessed on 28 June 2024).

[10]https://a16zcrypto.com/portfolio (accessed on 3 August 2023).

[11]https://lexdao.org/ (accessed on 3 August 2023).

on VitaDAO to fund and advance longevity research. Professionals in various fields are beginning to use DAOs to collaborate and achieve common goals. As of our writing (in August 2023), the Japanese government is creating a DAO to explore Web3 technology.[12] It is not inconceivable that professionals in the finance industry will go a similar path in future. DAOs are built on public blockchains or smart contract platforms, two terms that we use interchangeably in this book. We introduce what they are in the following chapter.

References

Bellavitis, C., Fisch, C., and Momtaz, P., 2023. The Rise of Decentralized Autonomous Organizations (DAOs): A First Empirical Glimpse. *Venture Capital*. https://www.tandfonline.com/doi/abs/10.1080/13691066.2022.21 16797.

Coase, R.H., 1937. The Nature of the Firm. *Economica*. https://onlinelibrary.wi ley.com/doi/10.1111/j.1468-0335.1937.tb00002.x.

De Filippi, P. and Hassan, S., 2016. Blockchain Technology as a Regulatory Technology: From Code is Law to Law is Code. *First Monday*. https:// firstmonday.org/ojs/index.php/fm/article/view/7113.

De Filippi, P. and Hassan, S., 2021. Decentralized Autonomous Organization. *Internet Policy Review* 10(2). https://policyreview.info/pdf/policyreview-2021-2-1556.pdf.

Desmarais-Tremblay, M., 2017. Musgrave, Samuelson, and the Crystallization of the Standard Rationale for Public Goods. *History of Political Economy*. https://read.dukeupress.edu/hope/article-abstract/49/1/59/12691/Musgr ave-Samuelson-and-the-Crystallization-of-the?redirectedFrom=fulltext.

Eisenhardt, K., 1989. Agency Theory: An Assessment and Review. *The Academy of Management Review*. https://www.jstor.org/stable/258191.

Fama, E., 1980. Agency Problems and the Theory of the Firm. *Journey of Political Economy*. https://www.jstor.org/stable/1837292.

Ferguson, N., 2009. *The Ascent of Money: A Financial History of the World*. https://www.niallferguson.com/the-ascent-of-money.

Ferguson, N., 2017. *The Square and the Tower*. https://www.niallferguson.com/ the-square-and-the-tower.

Galton, F., 1907. Vox Populi. *Nature*. https://www.nature.com/articles/075 450a0.

Hardin, G., 1968. The Tragedy of the Commons. *Science*. https://www.jstor.org/ stable/1724745.

---

[12]https://www.coindesk.com/policy/2022/11/03/japanese-digital-ministry-to-create-dao-for-web3-exploration (accessed on 3 August 2023).

Harari, Y., 2015. *Homo Deus: A Brief History of Tomorrow.* https://www.ynha
rari.com/book/homo-deus.

Jensen, M. and Meckling, W., 1976. Theory of the Firm: Managerial Behavior,
Agency Costs and ownership structure. *Journal of Financial Economics.*
https://www.sciencedirect.com/science/article/pii/0304405X7690026X.

Laloux, F., 2014. *Reinventing Organizations.* https://www.reinventingorganiza
tions.com.

Mehar, M., Shier, C., Giambattista, A., Gong, E., Fletcher, G., Sanayhie,
R., Kim, H., and Laskowski, M., 2019. Understanding a Revolutionary
and Flawed Grand Experiment in Blockchain: The DAO Attack. *Journal
of Cases on Information Technology.* https://www.igi-global.com/article/
understanding-a-revolutionary-and-flawed-grand-experiment-in-blockchain/
216950.

Morgan, G., 1986. *Images of Organization.* https://us.sagepub.com/en-us/nam/
images-of-organization/book229704.

Ostrom, E., 1990. *Governing the Commons.* https://www.amazon.com/Governing-
Commons-Evolution-Institutions-Collective/dp/1107569788.

Quinn, D., 2017. Experiments in Algorithmic Governance: A history and
ethnography of "The DAO", a failed Decentralized Organization. *Bitcoin and Beyond: Cryptocurrencies, Blockchains and Global Governance.* https://www.taylorfrancis.com/chapters/oa-edit/10.4324/9781315
211909-8/experiments-algorithmic-governance-quinn-dupont.

Ronfeldt, D., 1996. Tribes, Institutions, Markets, Networks: A Framework About
Societal Evolution. *Rand.* https://www.rand.org/content/dam/rand/pubs/
papers/2005/P7967.pdf.

Samuelson, P., 1954. The Pure Theory of Public Expenditure. *The Review of
Economics and Statistics.* https://www.jstor.org/stable/1925895.

Shleifer, A. and Vishny, R., 1997. A Survey of Corporate Governance. *The Journal
of Finance* https://onlinelibrary.wiley.com/doi/abs/10.1111/j.1540-6261.1
997.tb04820.x.

Surowiecki, J., 2005. *The Wisdom of Crowds.* https://www.penguinrandomhouse.
com/books/175380/the-wisdom-of-crowds-by-james-surowiecki/.

Ver Eecke, W., 1999. Public Goods: An Ideal Concept. *Journal of Socio-
Economics.* https://www.sciencedirect.com/science/article/pii/S10535357
99000049?via%3Dihub.

Von Neumann, J. and Morgenstern, O., 1944. *Theory of Games and Economic
Behavior.* https://press.princeton.edu/books/paperback/9780691130613/
theory-of-games-and-economic-behavior.

Chapter 2

Blockchains: The Operating Systems of DAOs

Abstract

This chapter explores the technical foundations and critical characteristics of blockchains and smart contract platforms. It defines blockchains, introduces the blockchain trilemma, and describes smart contract platforms as operating systems for building applications and governing organizations. The chapter delves into the characteristics critical to choosing a smart contract platform for building a decentralized autonomous organization (DAO), including transaction fees, stability, Turing completeness, reputation, energy consumption, privacy, fairness, and good governance. It provides detailed explanations, examples, and implications for each characteristic, emphasizing the importance of considering them holistically when selecting a blockchain. Ultimately, these characteristics can significantly impact a DAO's functionality, adoption, and long-term success and are essential for financial services professionals to understand before engaging DAOs.

2.1   What is a public blockchain?

There are many definitions of what a blockchain is. Functionally, Yermack's (2017) explanation is simple and on point: "A blockchain is a sequential database of information that is secured by methods of cryptographic proof, and it offers an alternative to classical financial ledgers." Bashir (2020) expanded the definition of a blockchain to "a peer-to-peer, distributed ledger that is cryptographically secure, append-only, immutable and updateable only via consensus or agreement amongst peers." We will break down what this definition means point by point.

The first is the concept of peer to peer. This suggests that in a transaction on a blockchain, there are no intermediaries involved. As most intermediaries charge a fee for their service, we expect transactions on a blockchain to be more cost-effective. In today's world of finance, there is always at least one intermediary between you and the person you are transacting with. As such, we incur plenty of charges. Examples of intermediaries include banks, custodians, clearinghouses, and exchanges. Second, the definition introduces a distributed ledger. A ledger is a collection of financial transactions or records. "Distributed" means many copies of this ledger are available on many computers on the blockchain network. Distributing updates to the nodes that host these copies of the ledger takes time. It is therefore logical that the processing speed of a distributed system is slower compared to a centralized system. But a blockchain is also more resilient since the failure of a single computer or node would not affect the network's overall health. Third, the definition mentions "cryptographically secure" as a blockchain property. This means transactions do not require trust in participants because they are cryptographically secured. This leads to the following essential part in Bashir's definition: "append-only, immutable, and only updateable via consensus." One of the reasons we can trust data stored on a blockchain is that once the data is recorded, it cannot be tampered with. Being tamper-proof is a crucial feature of ledgers that record financial transactions. Append-only means that new data can only be added sequentially. "Updateable via consensus" indicates there must be a mechanism to establish whether any new information is legitimate and agreed upon by consensus before being recorded onto a blockchain. We provide a more in-depth explanation of what a blockchain is in Appendix A.

Today, the enormous potential of blockchains is often overshadowed by the hype of cryptocurrency price action. However, as adoption by entrepreneurs and large corporations grows and use cases mature beyond speculation, we anticipate that the characteristics outlined in the following paragraphs will play a critical role for any DAO builder.

2.2 The blockchain trilemma

It is unclear who first came up with the blockchain trilemma concept. Three parties documented it in the same year. While there are some minor variations in the naming of the trilemma, Vitalik Buterin, the Founder of Ethereum; Will Cong, a Finance Professor at Cornell, and his coauthors (2021); and Markus Brunnermeier, a Professor of Economics at Princeton, and his coauthor Joseph Abadi from the Federal Reserve Bank of Philadelphia (2021) all documented the trilemma separately.[1]

At its core, the trilemma states that a decentralized ledger platform cannot simultaneously achieve high scalability, decentralization, and security. Scalability is about the platform's ability to handle a large number of transactions concurrently. A common measure of scalability is transaction per seconds (TPS). Decentralization can be measured in many ways, depending on the lens one analyses it through. Through a computer science lens, we count the number of nodes that validate transactions on a network. The economic wealth concentration of a network can also be a measure of decentralization. The third feature of security refers to the strength of resistance to adverse actors' attempts to manipulate the distributed ledger. Adverse actors are also known as "hackers." If all three features cannot be achieved simultaneously, then the user must decide which feature they prioritize as that would influence which blockchain platform to use.

---

[1]https://vitalik.eth.limo/general/2021/04/07/sharding.html (accessed on 25 July 2023).

2.3 Smart contract platforms and their adoptability characteristics

In 1997, cryptographer Nick Szabo introduced "the idea of smart contracts" in a piece with the same name title.[2] In it, he refers to an elementary form of a smart contract using a vending machine as an example. As we select and pay for a desired item in the machine, perhaps a chocolate bar, the contract is triggered and the bar is delivered to the user. Szabo was ahead of his time; in 1997, the internet and the digital realm were in their infancy. Today, the importance of smart contracts is more apparent as more critical activities are conducted online. In 2014, Vitalik Buterin created Ethereum, the first blockchain-based smart contract platform.[3] It was the first to allow its users to execute digital agreements in the form of code. Before Ethereum, decentralized systems like bitcoin were only able to make payments. With Ethereum, there is theoretically no limit to the utility applications developed on its platform and ecosystem.

What is a smart contract platform? One way of explaining it is to compare them to operating systems, such as MacOS, Unix, or Microsoft Windows. Application developers build their logic and user-facing systems on top of these platforms.

According to market data platform Messari, over 192 such smart contract platforms exist at the time of writing in mid-2023.[4] Our view is that not all of them will survive, but there will not be one dominant winner either. Potential use cases may be diverse and so are the characteristics of the platforms. While we explain characteristics in more detail throughout this chapter, some prominent examples

---

[2] https://www.fon.hum.uva.nl/rob/Courses/InformationInSpeech/CDROM/Lite rature/LOTwinterschool2006/szabo.best.vwh.net/idea.html (accessed on 26 July 2023).

[3] https://www.weusecoins.com/assets/pdf/library/Ethereum_white_paper-a_next_ generation_smart_contract_and_decentralized_application_platform-vitalik-buter in.pdf (accessed on 26 July 2023).

[4] https://messari.io/screener/screen/network-tokens-fh26 (accessed on 26 July 2023).

of smart contract platforms include Algorand, with its Pure Proof-of-Stake consensus mechanism and Turing incompleteness, which will be particularly attractive for use cases in financial services.[5,6] Solana with its high transaction throughput may be a good choice for large-scale online gaming with thousands of players, and Tezos being forkless and having implemented mechanisms to prevent programming errors (e.g. "formal verification" could be a superior choice for use cases where tolerance for error is particularly low, e.g. health care.)[7-9] Some of the use cases that have gotten initial traction are decentralized finance (or DeFi), gaming, and non-fungible tokens representing, for example, digital art. Smart contract platforms are also the operating systems for DAOs.

In the following sections, we will discuss the characteristics of smart contract platforms in detail. Note that we use the terms smart contract platform and blockchain interchangeably throughout the book. In addition to the widely discussed blockchain trilemma of security, transaction speed, and decentralization, there are also other characteristics that we believe will be significant. How transaction fees are handled, the stability of the platform, its Turing completeness, the reputation of the builders, its energy consumption, privacy-preserving features, and fair treatment of users as well as its governance are also critical to assess.

2.4 Low and predictable transaction fees

A coin or token is often embedded in these smart contract platforms, and one of the purposes of this native currency is to pay for transactions. Transactions can be simple value transfers from one

---

[5]https://algorand.com/technology/pure-proof-of-stake (accessed on 3 August 2023).

[6]https://www.coindesk.com/tech/2019/11/22/algorand-20s-new-non-turing-complete-smart-contracts-are-a-feature-not-a-bug/ (accessed on 3 August 2023).

[7]https://explorer.solana.com (accessed on 3 August 2023).

[8]https://www.reddit.com/r/tezos/comments/wsd8ay/explain_why_forkless_upgrades_are_a_big_thing (accessed on 3 August 2023).

[9]https://opentezos.com/formal-verification/modeling-theorem/ (accessed on 3 August 2023).

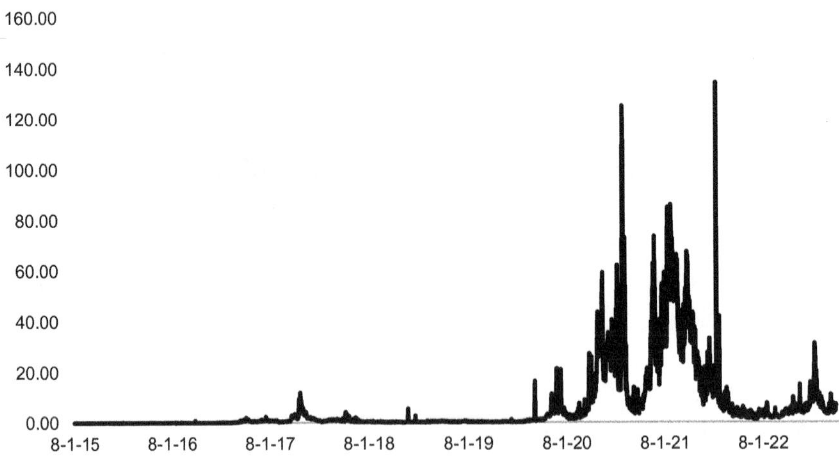

Fig. 2.1. Ethereum gas fees. Average daily transaction fee price in USD from August 2015 to end August 2022.

Source: https://etherscan.io/chart/gasprice (accessed on 26 July 2023).

wallet to another. Or they can be more complex and involve the execution of smart contracts. For example, swapping one token for a different token, or taking out a stablecoin loan against which one may have to deposit another cryptocurrency as collateral in the contract. What would be some basic requirements concerning fees on smart contract platforms? Low pricing and predictability.

Belleflamme and Peitz (2021) explain how platforms can increase volume by lowering transaction-related fees. In a competitive environment, and all else being equal, users will optimize for low transaction costs. Low transaction costs are relevant for keeping existing platform users and attaining new ones. One much-discussed application for blockchain technology is that of financial inclusion in developing countries. This involves micro-payments that established financial institutions cannot process at attractive rates. For a smart contract platform to be adopted in such environments, the transaction fees must be as low as a few cents. Some platforms excel in this context, and some do not score very well. With Figures 2.1 and 2.2, and Table 2.1, we compare transaction fees for Ethereum and

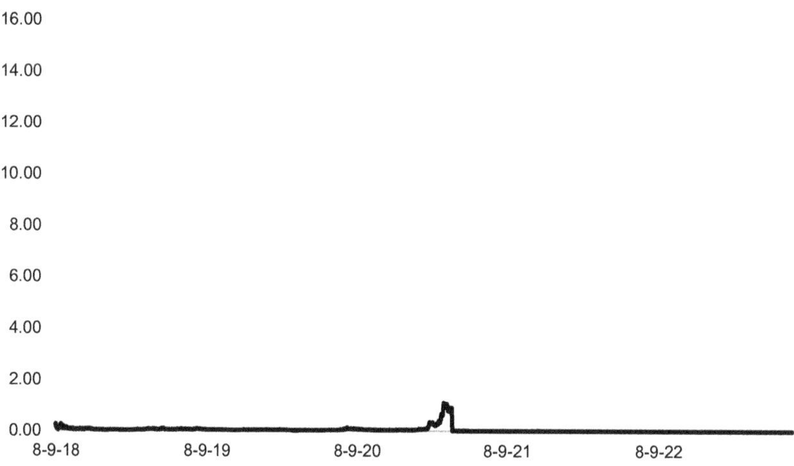

Fig. 2.2. vechain gas fees. Average daily transaction fee price in USD from August 2015 to end August 2022.

Source: vechainstats.com team. We thank Fabian and Paul for their swift support with our custom query.

Table 2.1. Descriptive statistics for average daily transaction fees in USD for the period 1 August 2015 to 24 July 2023 (Ethereum) and 9 August 2018 to 26 July 2023 (vechain).

	Ethereum	**vechain**
Mean	6.22	0.04
Standard error	0.24	0.00
Median	0.72	0.02
Minimum	0	0.00
Maximum	134.12	1.11
Count	2885	1814

Source: vechain (vechainstats.com team); Ethereum (https://etherscan.io/chart/gasprice, accessed on 26 July 2023).

Note: We thank Fabian and Paul for their swift support with our custom query.

vechain platforms, showing that vechain has much lower transaction fees than Ethereum.

Figures 2.1 and 2.2 also highlight another challenge: The predictability of transaction fees varies across platforms. Predictable transaction fees are critical for anyone who needs to manage the costs of their ongoing activities. This would include entrepreneurs, corporates, and financial institutions. Transaction costs affect many aspects of management: from the pricing of products to budgeting and forecasting, as well as competitive analysis. A question right now might be: Why is the variance of transaction fees high on one platform and low on the other smart contract platform? The difference is a result of a design choice. Ethereum deployed the concept of a gas auction where users can bid the price up, while on vechain, the price per transaction is based on a predefined amount that can only be changed through a governance process.[10]

2.5 Stability

A blockchain is a decentralized network of computer nodes and should by default be available, or as computer scientists call it "live" 365/24/7 (Alpern and Schneider, 1985). As such, it seems counterintuitive to question the stability of blockchains. The Bitcoin network is a good example, we are not aware of any meaningful outage since it was launched on 3 January 2009. That is not always the case with other platforms. In 2022, one of the largest smart contract platforms, Solana, suffered a series of outages where the service was severely degraded and transactions were not processed with regular performance.[11] On other occasions, the entire network shut down as nodes stopped validating transactions completely. Regulators are not yet stipulating "uptime" for services in the world of public blockchains. At the same time, users of smart contract platforms expect them to function seamlessly. Smart contract platforms are like Amazon's AWS or Google Cloud where we have extremely high expectations of the services. To illustrate, we use an example of a

---

[10]https://docs.vechain.org/thor/learn/transaction-calculation (accessed on 3 August 2023).

[11]Galaxy provides a timeline for some of the outages on this website: https://www.galaxy.com/research/whitepapers/surveying-solana (accessed on 10 July 2023).

borrower on a decentralized finance application. She deposits an asset as collateral which she is allowed to borrow against. If her collateral price drops below a certain level, she will get liquidated. During an outage, the price of her collateral drops below the critical threshold. Normally, she would access the platform and add collateral. However, the outage prevents her from doing so, and she gets liquidated when the platform resumes its service.

Let us now compare how a financial regulator handles the stability of components of their ecosystem. In Singapore, the Monetary Authority of Singapore issued the Technology Risk Management Guidelines that assist regulated financial services firms with how to manage their technology stack.[12] Under the Guidelines, banking institutions of systemic size have a 4-hour window of outage tolerance per year. Centralized entities often deploy intelligent high availability (HA) technology solutions to comply with such stringent requirements. Any outage that affects the general public will trigger the regulator's followup for the institution.

When choosing a smart contract platform to build a DAO, we recommend assessing the history of the platform in question to assess its stability.

2.6   Reputation

In a fully decentralized ecosystem based on cryptographic proofs, the reputation of different actors should not matter. However, reputation is essential in today's blockchain ecosystems, which are often more centralized than we assume. Saengchote *et al.* (2022) find that market participants still place trust in specific, known actors. As these blockchains evolve from their current experimental state into real-world public infrastructure, a framework to establish and evaluate their reputation is necessary, particularly for financial institutions. The pseudonymous nature of blockchains presents a challenge when assessing actors' credibility and trustworthiness. A multidimensional

---

[12]https://www.mas.gov.sg/regulation/guidelines/technology-risk-management-guidelines (accessed on 10 July 2023).

approach to managing different forms of reputational risk is required to comply with the tight regulatory environment faced by banks and other institutions. We will review the various forms of reputational risk starting with that of the creators and core developer teams. The credibility and motivations of founders and core developer teams form a significant factor of reputational risk. Exemplary creator groups are driven not by hubristic desires to crown themselves as the next "Crypto Titan" but by a genuine devotion to unlocking blockchains' potential for decentralized economic activity. Their focus is on fostering adoption and organic network growth — not rampant rent-seeking or speculative trading. The Ethereum community is one such positive example: they focus on building critical infrastructure and technology roadmaps to propel their platform forward. The ethos is one of humble building over blatant self-promotion. In contrast, creators with dubious reputation fixate on extracting personal wealth and clout. These questionable teams surround themselves with paid influencers rather than genuine subject matter experts who can add substance. Roadmaps prioritize rent-seeking business models, and it is not unheard of that teams engage in speculative asset pumps and other types of market manipulation of their own token. Teams like Tron appear to exemplify the reputational pitfalls of misaligned incentives, outsized egos, and the absence of sound stewardship of the ecosystem's evolution.[13]

The second form of reputation comes from the platform's user base. A positive user reputation results from communities engaging in meaningful discussions about technical topics, real-world use cases, and the platform's ongoing development. These ecosystems attract diverse participants, including corporations, universities, and even governments, whose presence lends further legitimacy to the platform. The Polkadot community exemplifies positive traits, focusing on substantive discourse and a varied, reputable user base.

---

[13]https://www.theverge.com/c/22947663/justin-sun-tron-cryptocurrency-polo niex (accessed on 6 May 2024).

In contrast, negative user reputations emerge when the community is dominated by speculative discussions and meme-driven hype, with little attention paid to the underlying technology or its practical applications. In these ecosystems, the user base consists primarily of individuals seeking quick profits rather than long-term value creation. It is imperative that the user base is not associated with illicit activities, questionable behavior, or sanctioned entities. The BNB Chain community, for instance, has faced criticism for its emphasis on speculation and the prevalence of users engaged in high-risk, short-term trading strategies.

Another way of gauging a project's reputation is via social media sentiment. Positive sentiment on platforms such as Twitter/X, Reddit, and Discord can indicate a thriving community, with users actively engaging in constructive discussions, sharing news and updates, and expressing enthusiasm for the ecosystem's potential. Such positive sentiment often correlates with a strong developer community and growing adoption. Conversely, negative sentiment, characterized by widespread criticism, skepticism, hostility, or other unprofessional and disrespectful behavior, can signal the underlying issues or controversies that may harm the ecosystem's reputation. These issues could range from technical problems and security breaches to concerns about centralization, lack of transparency, or misalignment with the original vision. Various tools and methods can be employed to analyze social media sentiment, such as natural language processing algorithms and sentiment analysis APIs.

Manual monitoring of critical channels and influencers is also very valuable. However, it is crucial to recognize the limitations of relying solely on social media sentiment, as factors such as echo chambers, manipulated narratives, or short-term hype can influence it. As such, while social media sentiment provides valuable insights, it should be considered alongside other factors, such as creator and user reputations, to comprehensively assess a blockchain ecosystem's overall reputation. In summary, evaluating these forms of reputation holistically is essential for mitigating the reputational risk of the platform on which the DAO chooses to build on.

2.7 Energy consumption

In the world of blockchains, energy consumption is a contentious issue. Proponents of the Bitcoin network and its Proof-of-Work (PoW) consensus mechanism argue that its energy consumption is worth its value. Opponents disagree and say that its energy consumption is not justified and unsustainable. DAOs, however, build on platforms that use a different consensus mechanism, Proof-of-Stake (PoS). When the largest smart contract platform, Ethereum, migrated from PoW to PoS, its energy consumption fell by 99.95%. The next level of sophistication in energy consumption measurement will be comparing smart contract platforms at a more granular level.

We encourage DAO founders to make energy consumption one of the characteristics to evaluate when choosing a platform to build on.

2.8 Privacy

Privacy matters. In a seminal paper from 1993, long before Satoshi invented what we today know as a blockchain, one of the godfathers of the Cypherpunk movement, Berkeley Professor Eric Hughes, explained in his manifesto that Cypherpunks "write software to defend privacy".[14] Cypherpunks are very determined about their mission; they will not stop because others disagree with their goals. Privacy matters in personal life when doing business and interacting with government bodies. One of the prominent features of a public blockchain is that anyone can view the ledger and transaction details between blockchain addresses. The visibility of transactions on a blockchain raises potential problems as there are often legitimate reasons for wanting to keep transaction details private.

Government agencies worldwide have made clear that they want the distributed ledger technology to be transparent and inspectable. To counter money laundering activities, the US Department of the

---

[14]https://www.activism.net/cypherpunk/manifesto.html (accessed on 12 October 2023).

Treasury Financial Crimes Enforcement Network issued what is commonly known as the "travel rule".[15] Since 1997, it "requires all financial institutions to pass on certain information to the next financial institution, in certain funds transmittals involving more than one financial institution." Crypto intermediaries such as exchanges, custodians, and brokers that provide access to blockchain platforms must comply with this rule. The mandatory implementation of the travel rule by regulated crypto exchanges and custodians includes mapping their user base to wallet addresses and asking users to declare that they control the wallet they withdraw funds to. When the travel rule is applied widely, capital flows across blockchain networks are traceable. As such, it limits the privacy of users.

Another recent example of governments' appetite for transparency is the 2023 persecution of the founders of the smart contract-based Tornado Cash platform.[16] Tornado Cash is a blockchain-based mixer that enables users to obfuscate fund flows by using a decentralized finance primitive — a liquidity pool that effectively disassociates the funds from the depositor and the wallet address withdrawing the funds. The allegations against the founders Roman Storm and Roman Semenov include support of criminal activity in the form of sanction evasion and money laundering.[17] In May 2024, Tornado Cash developer Alexy Pertsev was sentenced to 64 months in jail for money laundering by the Dutch court.

While mixing flows in traditional finance carries negative connotations, on a blockchain, there are strong and sound reasons for using mixers to protect privacy. As highlighted in a blog post, privacy protection requirements are and will continue to be driven

---

[15] https://www.fincen.gov/sites/default/files/advisory/advissu7.pdf (accessed on 12 October 2023).

[16] https://berkeley-defi.github.io/assets/material/Tornado%20Cash%20White paper.pdf (accessed on 12 October 2023).

[17] https://www.justice.gov/usao-sdny/pr/tornado-cash-founders-charged-money-laundering-and-sanctions-violations (accessed on 12 October 2023).

by two forces: security and regulation.[18] "Imagine how a country's security could be affected if friends and foes alike could monitor its reserves in real time. How an individual's personal security could be compromised if would-be kidnappers could track their wealth. How a company's fortunes or stock price might fare if competitors and shareholders could view its investments and free cash flows at any given time. Or how a foundation that provides financial support to a persecuted minority could be targeted by others able to access information on its disbursements." The second force is regulation. In many jurisdictions, there is regulation to protect entities' privacy. Examples include the European Union with the General Data Protection Regulation (GDPR) and Singapore with the Personal Data Protection Act (PDPA). There is constant tension between the individual right to privacy and the regulatory pressure for surveillance.

Currently, we are far from consensus on the desired balance. To illustrate the divergence in current thinking regarding privacy, we share an anecdote: One of the authors attended a closed-door meeting in 2022 with high-ranking government officials from different nations and a community of crypto entrepreneurs. The opinions could not have been more diverse when the conversation turned to privacy. "The only thing Satoshi got wrong in the Bitcoin Whitepaper is that he made the ledger inspectable by everyone," said one entrepreneur of a highly valued crypto startup. Government officials countered in various ways — they must persecute bad actors, criminals, and terrorists and therefore need full transparency. Suddenly, the room went silent. A cryptographer sitting in the corner of the room, who had been very quiet during the previous 90 minutes, asked to speak and instantly grabbed everyone's attention. We are paraphrasing here, but his message was quite clear: Protection of privacy and making distributed ledgers transparent are not two ends of a spectrum. Instead, he invited us to learn

---

[18]https://realise.asia/give-me-some-privacy-how-blockchains-can-achieve-mass-adoption (accessed on 12 October 2023).

more about cryptographic primitives, such as Zero-Knowledge-Proofs (ZKP), Multiparty Computation (MPC), and fully homomorphic encryption (FHE):

- ZKPs are methods by which one party — the prover — can prove to another part — the verifier — that a given statement is true based on underlying data that does not need to be disclosed.[19] Think of a bartender who only needs to know whether a customer is at least 21 years old to buy alcohol, rather than having to know their exact birthdate.
- MPC methods enable parties to jointly compute a function through inputs while those inputs remain private.[20] The "millionaires' problem," in which two rich people want to find out who is richer without giving away additional information about their wealth, is an often-cited scenario to explain the utility of MPC.
- FHE enables users to perform computations on encrypted data without first decrypting it.[21] This method permits, for example, a company to crowdsource a credit rating from many data scientists without having to reveal its balance sheet data to everyone.[22]

We are confident that more privacy-preserving technology will be used in future, particularly for platforms powering DAOs. We expect that creative cryptographers and entrepreneurs will deliver platforms that can satisfy privacy protection requirements and give cryptographic certainty to regulators and law enforcement agencies.

---

[19] https://people.csail.mit.edu/silvio/Selected%20Scientific%20Papers/Proof%20Systems/The_Knowledge_Complexity_Of_Interactive_Proof_Systems.pdf (accessed on 12 October 2023).

[20] https://ieeexplore.ieee.org/abstract/document/4568388 (accessed on 12 October 2023).

[21] https://eprint.iacr.org/2015/1192 (accessed on 12 October 2023).

[22] https://www.synnax.ai (accessed on 15 May 2024).

2.9 Fairness

None of us wants to be treated unfairly by others. This is true in both the physical and digital world. But what is fairness? Broome (1984, 1991) provides a foundational understanding, asserting that it involves comparing how well everyone's claims are met relative to others. Kahneman and colleagues' research in 1986 reveals that fairness significantly influences economic behavior. Firms and individuals will likely reject inequitable transactions and avoid engaging with those who act unfairly. What is particularly notable in Kahneman *et al.*'s findings is that participants in the experiments acted on fairness principles anonymously. In the blockchain context, we often deal with pseudonymous or, at times, even anonymous actors. Therefore, the Nobel Prize winners' insights are hugely relevant.[23] They suggest that maintaining fairness with stakeholders is critical to remaining competitive. We believe this finding will influence DAO builders when choosing which blockchain to adopt in future.

How do we assess and compare blockchain platforms on fair collaboration? Li *et al.* (2023) explore this question by examining how some validators influence the order of transactions in a distributed ledger and its resulting financial implications. Daian *et al.* (2019) exemplify this fairness-related issue by highlighting the issue of maximum extractable value (MEV). MEV is an activity where some blockchain validators manipulate the transaction order to their benefit and the detriment of regular users. The process of exploiting MEV is twofold: first, the rogue validator identifies arbitrage opportunities, and second, they bid up the fees to execute the related transaction. The result is excessive fees incurred by ordinary users on networks like Ethereum. While eliminating such practices completely may not be possible, some suggest that reducing the time available for these activities could lessen their occurrence.

Since DAO members directly pay transaction costs on smart contract platforms, we believe DAO builders must consider

---

[23]We explain the differences between pseudonymous and anonymous in Section 4.2.2 of Chapter 4, under the membership header.

fairness-related characteristics when choosing a platform to build on. Macpherson (2023) identifies the critical nature of predictable transaction outcomes for blockchain adoption. Further research by Alpos *et al.* (2023) and Chen *et al.* (2023) address the issue of unfair trading practices, suggesting that the ability of validators to prioritize their transactions is a flaw in blockchain systems. Guo (2023) adds to this discussion by proposing that reducing blockchain block times could limit MEV opportunities, thus promoting fairness.

Fairness, like other characteristics discussed in this chapter, influences adoption. We posit that in the future, smart contract platforms that make unfair behavior more difficult will outperform the ones where average users are easily exploited.

We recommend building DAOs on smart contract platforms that allow for relatively less unfair behavior to grow their member base successfully.

2.10 Good governance

As the blockchain industry matures, the question of what constitutes good governance in these decentralized ecosystems has become increasingly critical. Werbach *et al.* (2024) analyze 23 blockchain projects and shed light on the current state of governance and the challenges that may lie ahead. The article offers five essential insights: on-chain/off-chain governance balance, explicit formalization of rules, legitimacy, and pragmatic approach to decentralization.

The first finding relates to optimizing off-chain and on-chain governance mechanisms. Off-chain governance, which includes the actions of stakeholders, leaders, and DAO-associated legal entities like foundations and companies, plays a vital role in guiding the direction of projects and facilitating coordination. These processes must be transparent and accountable to the broader community. On-chain governance, which is implemented through token-based voting, allows for the direct participation of stakeholders in decision-making and helps align incentives. The most effective governance systems leverage the strengths of both off-chain and on-chain mechanisms while mitigating their weaknesses. The willingness to embrace both on-chain and off-chain governance is fundamentally different from those who believe that a DAO's governance must be fully on-chain. As part of the latter group, Rikken *et al.* (2023) define DAOs as "a system in which storage and transaction of value and notary (voting) functions can be designed, organized, recorded, and archived and where data and actions are recorded and autonomously executed in a decentralized way."

Another critical aspect of good governance is formalizing rules and procedures. While blockchain technology aims to reduce reliance on centralized authorities, even decentralized systems require agreed-upon rules to function effectively. Projects can enhance transparency, predictability, and fairness by formalizing governance processes. This includes clearly defining the roles and powers of different stakeholder groups, establishing decision-making criteria, and outlining dispute resolution mechanisms.

Good governance also involves establishing and maintaining legitimacy in the eyes of the community. Legitimacy can be derived from various sources, such as adherence to the smart contract platform's original vision, successful voting processes, or the endorsement of reputable entities. Blockchains with legitimacy are better positioned to navigate crises, make difficult decisions, and adapt to changing circumstances.

Finally, good governance recognizes that decentralization is not an end to itself but a means to create resilient, adaptable, and sustainable ecosystems that deliver value to users and stakeholders. Progressive decentralization, where projects gradually distribute power and control over time, can effectively balance the benefits of centralized coordination with the robustness of decentralized networks. It will, therefore, be interesting to study decentralization characteristics outlined by Kitzler *et al.* (2023) and Feichtinger *et al.* (2023) in the future, when more data are available, to monitor smart contract platforms' progress in this regard.

We recommend that DAO builders and their communities select blockchain platforms with good governance to reduce associated risks.

2.11 Turing completeness

Turing completeness deserves a closer look as a core technical trait of blockchains. It directly relates to the architecture and programming language powering smart contract platforms and is somewhat controversial. While some say Turing-complete platforms are powerful, others argue that they have severe limitations. Turing completeness is one of the most technically complex aspects of our book.

We need to revisit a few foundational thinkers to set the stage. The first is Kurt Gödel, an early 20th-century Austrian logician, whose incompleteness theorems exposed the inherent limitations of any formal mathematical system, including those that will subsequently be used in smart contract platforms. Gödel demonstrated that there will always be true statements that cannot be proven within a given set of axioms and rules. No matter how comprehensive, there are unavoidable gaps where truth exists but cannot be formally derived from within the defined system itself. Gödel's insights had profound ripple effects across logic, computer science, philosophy, and our understanding of the constraints on any computational model.

Next is Alan Turing, the British pioneer of modern computing, whose work on algorithms and computational theory was groundbreaking. Turing completeness refers to the ability of a system, like a programming language, to perform any possible computation that a machine can undertake. It is akin to having an infinitely flexible set of building blocks to construct any structure you can conceptualize. Languages like Python or Java are Turing-complete — equipped with features like loops and conditionals (if, then, and else) that empower them to solve any computational problem. This power is appealing for smart contract platforms aiming to be versatile digital infrastructure for peer-to-peer commerce. It may even be advantageous to some DAOs.

However, Turing completeness is a double-edged sword, as it exposes the "halting problem" that Gödel identified. Turing-complete machines can run self-referential programs that create paradoxical scenarios where predictability breaks down regarding whether

Table 2.2. Turing completeness.

No.	Platform	Turing complete	Programming language
1	Ethereum	Yes	Solidity
2	Bitcoin	No	Script
3	Cardano	Yes	Haskell/Marlowe
4	Binance Smart Chain	Yes	Solidity
5	Polkadot	No	Rust/Substrate
6	Solana	No	Rust
7	Ripple/XRP	No	N/A
8	Avalanche	Yes	Solidity
9	Cosmos	No	Wasm
10	Algorand	No	TEAL
11	Tezos	Yes	LIGO
12	Tron	Yes	Solidity
13	EOS	Yes	C++
14	Filecoin	No	Wasm
15	vechain	No	Various
16	Chainlink	No	Solidity
17	Stellar	No	Soroban
18	NEO	Yes	Various
19	Monero	No	N/A
20	IOTA	No	Various

computation will cease or continue indefinitely. There are tangible risks that blockchains built with Turing-complete languages must wrestle with:

- security vulnerabilities from code complexity;
- inefficiency and scalability woes from intensive computation;
- lack of predictability from the halting problem;
- regulatory uncertainties with such flexible infrastructure;
- upgrade/maintenance challenges from the intricate dependencies.

Cutting-edge platforms like Aptos and Sui are pioneering the novel "Move" language, aiming to be Turing-complete while mitigating some of these drawbacks — though their viability remains unproven today. Ultimately, the double-edged nature of Turing completeness exemplifies the intricate technical balancing acts blockchain

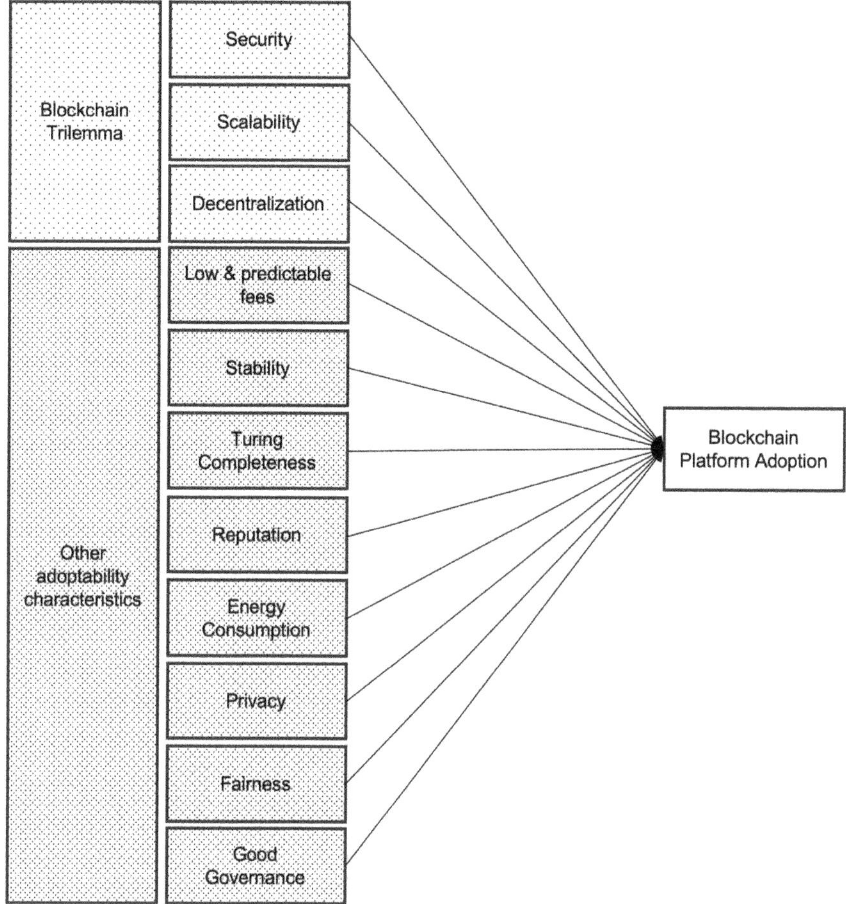

Fig. 2.3. Blockchain adoptability.

adopters face on the path to meeting enterprise-grade demands (Table 2.2).

For DAOs that plan to implement complex logic into their smart contracts, carefully evaluating worst-case scenarios because of Turing completeness and understanding possible effects are advisable.

To conclude, the blockchain platforms are DAOs' operating systems. Currently, the adoption of blockchains and the DAO concept is low. But since DAOs might have millions of members in future, understanding the adoptability characteristics of the underlying smart contract platforms is important (Fig. 2.3). For financial services professionals, this chapter helps in understanding underlying technologies used by DAOs. In Chapter 3, we turn to DAO governance.

References

Abadi, J. and Brunnermeier, M., 2021. Blockchain Economics. *Working Paper*. https://markus.scholar.princeton.edu/sites/g/files/toruqf2651/files/blockchain_paper_v11f.pdf.

Alpern, B. and Schneider, F., 1985. Defining Liveness. *Information Processing Letters*. https://doi.org/10.1016/0020-0190(85)90056-0.

Alpos, O., Cachin, C., Amores-Sesar, I., and Yeo, M., 2023. Eating Sandwiches: Modular and Lightweight Elimination of Transaction Reordering Attacks. *arXiv Electronic Journal*. https://arxiv.org/pdf/2307.02954.pdf.

Bashir, I., 2020. *Mastering Blockchain*, Third Edition. https://www.packtpub.com/product/mastering-blockchain-third-edition/9781839213199.

Belleflamme, P. and Peitz, M., 2021. *The Economics of Platforms*. Cambridge University Press. https://doi-org.eur.idm.oclc.org/10.1017/9781108696913.

Broome, J., 1984. Uncertainty and Fairness. *The Economic Journal*. https://doi.org/10.2307/2232707.

Broome, J., 1990. Fairness. *Proceedings of the Aristotelian Society*. http://www.jstor.org/stable/4545128.

Chen, J., Wang, Y., Zhou, Y., Ding, W., Tang, Y., Wang, X., and Li, K., 2023. Understanding the Security Risks of Decentralized Exchanges by Uncovering Unfair Trades in the Wild. *Working Paper*. https://tristartom.github.io/docs/eurosp23.pdf.

Chen, L., Cong, W., and Xiao, Y., 2021. A Brief Introduction to Blockchain Economics. *Information for Efficient Decision Making*. https://www.worldscientific.com/doi/abs/10.1142/9789811220470_0001.

Daian, P., Goldfeder, S., Kell, T., Li, Y., Bentov, I., Breidenbach, L., and Juels, A., 2019. Flashboys 2.0: Frontrunning, Transaction Reordering, and Consensus Instability in Decentralized Exchanges. *Working Paper. https://arxiv.org/abs/1904.05234*.

Feichtinger, R., Fritsch, R., Vonlanthen, Y., and Wattenhofer, R., 2023. The Hidden Shortcomings of (D)AOs — An Empirical Study of On-Chain Governance. *Working Paper*. https://arxiv.org/pdf/2302.12125.pdf.

Guo, A., 2023. Invariance Properties of Maximal Extractable Value. *Working Paper*. https://arxiv.org/abs/2304.11010.

Kahneman, D., Knetsch, J. L., and Thaler, R. H., 1986. Fairness and the Assumptions of Economics. *The Journal of Business*. http://www.jstor.org/stable/2352761.

Kitzler, S., Balietti, S., Saggese, P., Haslhofer, B., and Strohmaier, M., 2023. The Governance of Decentralized Autonomous Organizations: A Study of

Contributors' Influence, Networks, and Shifts in Voting Power. *Working Paper.* https://arxiv.org/abs/2309.14232.

Li, R., Hu, X., Wang, Q., Duan, S., and Wang, Q., 2023. Transaction Fairness in Blockchains, Revisited. Cryptology ePrint Archive. https://eprint.iacr.org/2023/1034.

Macpherson, A.W., 2023. Adversarial Blockchain Queues and Trading on a CFMM. *Working Paper.* https://arxiv.org/abs/2302.01663.

Rikken, O., Janssen, M., and Roosenboom-Kwee, Z., 2023. Governance Impacts of Blockchain-based Decentralized Autonomous Organizations: An Empirical Analysis. *Policy Design and Practice.* https://pure.tudelft.nl/ws/portal files/portal/161113463/Governance_impacts_of_blockchain_based_decentrali zed_autonomous_organizations_an_empirical_analysis.pdf.

Saengchote, K., Putniņš, P., and Samphantharak, K., 2022. Does DeFi Remove the Need for Trust? Evidence from a Natural Experiment in Stablecoin Lending. *Working Paper.* https://arxiv.org/abs/2207.06285.

Werbach, K., De Filippi, P., Tan, J., and Pieters, G., 2024. Blockchain Governance in the Wild. *Cryptoeconomic Systems Journal.* https://cryptoecono micsystems.pubpub.org/pub/blockchain-governance-wild/release/1.

Yermack, D., 2017. Corporate Governance and Blockchains. *Review of Finance.* https://doi.org/10.1093/rof/rfw074.

Chapter 3

DAO Governance and Dispute Resolution

Abstract

This chapter explores the governance processes and voting rights crucial to the success of decentralized autonomous organizations (DAOs). It breaks down governance into agenda setting, voting, execution, and dispute resolution. The chapter discusses the decentralized nature of agenda setting in DAOs, voting models, eligibility criteria, incentive mechanisms, and consensus rules. It also addresses proposal execution challenges and the friction between the physical world and the blockchain. Finally, it explores dispute resolution mechanisms, including decentralized dispute resolution systems (DDRS), comparing them based on cost, efficiency, and compatibility.

3.1   Setting the scene

In Chapter 1, we reviewed some definitions of a DAO. We noted some common characteristics of DAOs, of which one is that DAOs run on top of public blockchains. As such, DAOs inherit some properties of blockchains: permissionlessness, transparency, decentralization, and cryptographic security. In our book, one of the requirements to qualify as a DAO is to have tokenized voting rights to conduct governance on a public blockchain. We believe that the design of sound governance processes and voting rights as coordination tools is central to the success of any DAO. Financial services professionals must understand how decision-making in DAOs works and what processes are agreed upon if a conflict arises. Assessing the governance

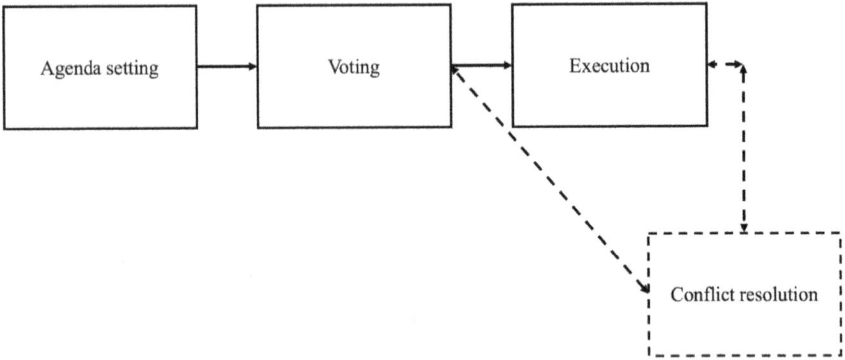

Fig. 3.1. Steps in the DAO governance process.

process of a DAO enables a financial services professional to make sounder decisions around counterparty risk. DAO governance is a swiftly evolving field for scholars across disciplines. We cite the relevant works where possible, but we also recognize that by the time we finish our manuscript, there will be new articles to complement our work. For example, Tan *et al.* (2023) elaborate on open problems in DAOs from the fields of computer science, economics, political science, and philosophy, opening research avenues in these fields pertaining to DAO governance. Due to the primacy of governance in DAOs, an entire chapter is dedicated to it. We review the steps of the governance process, which are agenda setting, voting, execution and dispute resolution (Fig. 3.1).

3.2 Agenda setting

We are familiar with the process of agenda setting from the corporate world: Usually, a board appointed by and representing shareholders in a company defines the agenda of a board meeting. Board members table meeting items that require shareholders to decide using the voting rights that are attached to the shares. Typically, boards need shareholder buy-in for significant M&A activity and changes to corporate structure, for example, amending the articles of association and issuing additional shares. Also, executive compensation, stock option plans, dividends, sale of significant amounts of assets, and changes in auditors require shareholder approval. Last, if there are decisions to be made about a possible bankruptcy or liquidation, and if shareholder rights are to change, then shareholders' approval is required. Shareholder rights are not all the same. Gompers *et al.* (2003) find that companies with the strongest shareholder rights earned an excess return of 8.5% during the researcher's sample period. Notably, the board members have the agenda-setting power since they control what decisions are put forward to the shareholders. In the corporate context, this right is exclusive to board members, although inputs from management, shareholders, regulators, and other government agencies can influence the agenda informally. It can be argued that the advantage of having a relatively small group of individuals decide what makes it onto the agenda is efficiency. This makes the proposal spam, a situation where many useless proposals are tabled more unlikely. On the other hand, a disadvantage is that decision-making power is very concentrated. As a small shareholder, it is not easy to influence the agenda. As Daron Acemoglu (2023) observes in his book *Power and Progress* regarding the effects of power structures, "whoever asks the questions, sets the priorities ... and has formidable powers to frame public discussion and convince others." The power of the board to set the agenda raises questions about the potential conflict of interests between board members and other stakeholders and shareholders.

In DAOs, we face a very different setup. In principle, anyone with the governance token can issue a proposal for fellow token holders to vote on. Comparatively, the agenda-setting process is much more decentralized and open than in the corporate setup. DAO governance encourages broad participation by token holders, but this opens the door for proposal spam where a rogue actor could substantially slow down the governance process by raising a massive number of nonsensical proposals. Such proposal spam would have detrimental effects on the decision-making capabilities of a DAO. To deter rogue actors from proposal spamming, DAOs can impose a cost for proposal submission. For example, the proposer must pay five tokens to submit in the Dash ecosystem. Some DAOs ask for a stake in a certain number of tokens for the duration of the proposal.

Others like Uniswap require the proposer to have substantial voting power delegated to them to ask governance token holders to vote on-chain (2.5 million UNI at the time of writing worth USD 16.125 million).

Challenges related to agenda setting include rogue actors making malicious proposals to benefit themselves at the cost of the DAO and a lack of expertise of the proposer. There are however ways to address these challenges. The Uniswap DAO has an excellent way to allow small token holders to gather community support through delegation before proposing a vote on an important matter. Without it, smaller token holders would be excluded from the process. A DAO could also categorize proposals and have different thresholds for different types of proposals to be as inclusive as possible. Delegation, which we will discuss in more detail under the voting section in this chapter, is also a valuable mechanism to ensure that experts propose sensible recommendations for voters to decide on. Delegates are ideally very familiar with the ins and outs of the protocol and, hence, can act as a valuable intermediary when making decisions to benefit the DAO collective. Additionally, if voters can establish the reputation of proposers, this will enable the community of voters to focus on proposals that come from a legitimate source.

Initial proposal discussions often happen on social media, such as Reddit or Discord, or a dedicated forum platform on the DAO website.[1] Often, time limits of several days are stipulated for the community to discuss and provide feedback during a period reserved for 'request for comment'. The feedback the proposer gathers at this stage must be included in subsequent steps of the governance process.

3.3 Voting

When reviewing the literature investigating corporate voting, we note that the agency issue between shareholders, board members and executives dominates the discussion. Yermack (2010) highlights that "Shareholders lack specific information about the firm, and their

---

[1]The Uniswap platform offers a forum on their website, https://gov.uniswap. org, where proposals can be discussed among community members.

voting decisions may depart from superior choices that managers, with better information, might make on their own." Nenova (2003) starts her article on the value of corporate control with the following: "Parties in control of a corporation are in a position to extract private benefits of control that do not accrue to dispersed shareholders." Following the framework by Ding *et al.* (2023), we discuss the following questions in the context of voting in a DAO:

- Who is entitled to vote?
- How does the voting process function?
- How is consensus established?
- What are the different voting models available?

3.3.1 *Who votes?*

Who gets to vote depends on the eligibility criteria set up by the DAO. Currently, there are three distinct eligibility criteria for voting in DAOs:

- one-token one-vote, where each token in a user's wallet represents a single vote;
- one-person-one-vote, where voting power is limited to one vote per wallet[2];
- restricted voting, where voting rules restrict decision-making to specific DAO members.

There are a few possible ways to implement restricted voting. (1) Members are required to hold a certain number of tokens, for example, in Dash DAO, a member needs at least 1000 Dash tokens to be able to vote in its ecosystem. (2) DAOs can enforce restrictions by evaluating the reputation of actors. Their reputation depends on the level of activity and other contributions in achieving the DAO's objectives, for example, contributing to smart contract code. The third form of restricted voting is delegation, where delegates get elected by nominators and then command their voting power.

---

[2]Due to the anonymous structure of public blockchains, it is technically possible that a single human controls multiple wallets.

The idea behind delegation is that small token holders often may not be qualified to make certain decisions or do not have the time to contribute. Hence, they elect a delegate by signing a transaction on the blockchain that delegates their voting power. Since nominators can revoke their delegation quickly, industry practitioners often call governance models based on delegation liquid democracy.

3.3.2 *The process*

"A DAO's voting process is comparable to a stockholders' meeting, where all eligible voters come together to vote on a proposal at hand. In a DAO, each voter will have one chance to vote. The vote cannot be reversed once immutably recorded on the blockchain. An advantageous characteristic of blockchain-based DAOs is that a proposal and its voting outcome can be inspected by others on the spot. However, a disadvantage is that not all eligible voters may participate in the process, leading to low turnout rates. Some DAOs have implemented a quorum to counter this issue of low turnout" (Ding *et al.*, 2023). Fritsch *et al.* (2022) document that less than 10% of token holders vote on proposals in the prominent DAOs: Uniswap, Compound and ENS (Fig. 3.2).

3.3.3 *Consensus*

When the DAO communities vote on proposals, outcomes are dependent on rules. These rules govern when the community can accept a proposal for subsequent deployment and execution of smart contract code. A simple majority is often required for a proposal to be accepted. Voters can support the proposal (Yes) or vote against it (No). They can also abstain and not participate. If the percentage of support for Yes supersedes the support or number of votes for No, the proposal is accepted, and the inverse is also true. Some governance systems implement a variation: the super-majority. A super-majority requires a specified minimum percentage of Yes-votes to pass the proposal. Additionally, governance designers may implement a quorum. A quorum requires a certain level of voter participation. The community will only accept the proposal if the

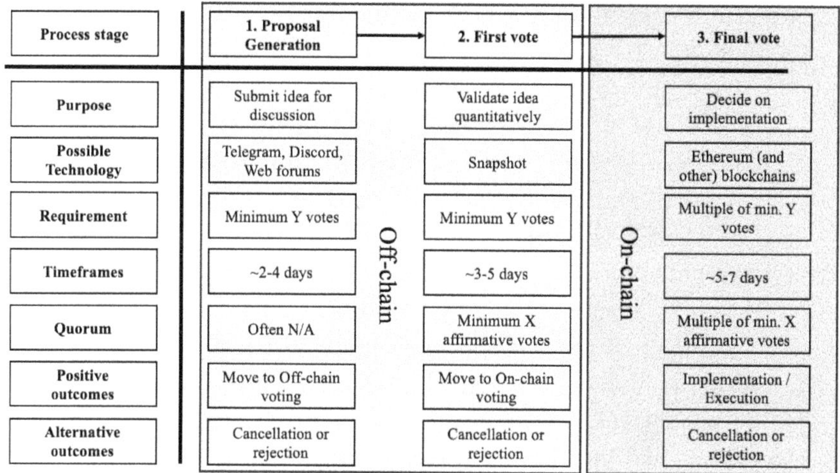

Fig. 3.2. Common DAO voting process.

defined level of voter participation is achieved, and the required majority supports the proposal.

3.3.4 *Voting models*

Ding *et al.* (2023) compare different voting models based on efficiency, fairness, scalability, robustness and check for the availability of incentive schemes:

(1) **Token-based quorum voting**: A quorum is a minimum number of participants that must take part in the vote on a specific proposal. Without quorums, single actors can take advantage of low participation to pursue their objectives. DAOs often implement quorums to ensure that there is wider representation and fewer chances of manipulation by a minority of members. Quorum requirements also help improve the legitimacy of decisions as decisions have been made by enough voters. This voting form is implemented by major players in the current DAO ecosystem, for example, Uniswap.

The UNI token can be used to participate in governance decisions on Uniswap. A detailed description of how UNI is used in Uniswap's governance process is detailed in a January 2023 update.[3] We summarize it here: The first stage in the governance process is a Request For Comment (RFC) on a proposal. After the community provides feedback, the process moves to the second phase which is a Temperature Check. At this stage, if the proposal garners the minimum required support, it moves to the next and final stage, the on-chain vote. If the proposal passes, it will be implemented.

(2) **Quadratic voting**: Instead of voters merely supporting or rejecting a proposal, quadratic voting allows them to express the intensity of their preferences through their votes. This type of voting enables voters with high conviction to impact the vote. First proposed by Lalley and Wey (2012), quadratic voting is based on the idea that each voter gets a budget to pay for votes. It allows for the "incorporation of intensity of preference and knowledge." The voter's budget might be USD 1,000. If she has high conviction and deep preference for a certain outcome, she will allocate a higher proportion of her budget to it. The rationale for quadratic voting is to address the limitations of the one-person–one-vote system which potentially can lead to tyranny of the majority. Quadratic voting allows for a more nuanced expression of preferences.

(3) **Weighted voting and reputation-based voting**: This form of voting considers voters' characteristics when weighing their vote. Characteristics could include the individual's reputation, contribution to the organization, or how many tokens they own. The objective is that those best positioned to contribute to the decision-making progress are given the required latitude in the process. Weighted voting, e.g. the one token–one vote model, is relatively common in today's DAOs. Reputation-based voting, implemented with soul-bound tokens that are non-transferable and tied to one individual only, is not very common yet and is currently at an experimental stage.

---

[3] *Source*: https://gov.uniswap.org/t/community-governance-process-update-jan-2023/19976 (accessed on 4 Dec 2023).

(4) **Knowledge-extractable voting (KEV)**: In this type of voting model, voters must either solve a puzzle or answer a question to be eligible to submit their vote. Implementing this type of feature in a voting process may prevent Sybil attacks where an adverse actor uses multiple addresses to spam the system, thus manipulating voting outcomes or breaking the voting process entirely. In the context of a blockchain-based DAO, this approach makes a lot of sense, particularly if we are missing a decentralized identity (DiD) system that reliably solves such attacks.

(5) **Multi-sig voting**: This adds an additional layer of approval to the voting process. Once the community has voted on a proposal, signatories can approve a transaction on the blockchain jointly using multi-sig technology. Many decentralization purists do not like the idea of dependence on a few key holders; they see it as a form of centralized control. Effectively, multi-sig key holders become the gatekeepers or intermediaries in the governance process. Voters in a system that depends on multi-sig-related processes must understand this nuance. Eventually, having more than one individual sign off on a particular decision reduces collusion risk. On the other hand, the few individuals with the keys can also ignore the voting outcome of the larger population of voters and do as they please.

(6) **Holographic consensus**: This aims to address the issue that not all DAO token holders need to participate in all decisions. Where the scope of the decision affects only a subset of the DAO, holographic voting allows decisions to be taken in smaller groups. In this context, relative majority, which is having a majority among only those who vote will enable swifter decision-making. Note that this concept is opposite to that of the quorum.

(7) **Conviction voting**: In this type of voting, voters must stake their governance tokens, or voting rights, to the decision, and as such, tokens become non-transferable until a specified time. This could be until a quorum is reached, or the voting outcome is clear. This form of voting also deters bad actors from manipulating the voting process as they would forego their staked amount if

Table 3.1. Voting types.

	Efficiency	Fairness	Scalability	Robustness	Incentive schemes
Token-based quorum voting	Medium	High	Low	Low	Not
Quadratic voting	Medium	Low	Medium	Medium	Not
Weighted voting and reputation-based voting	Medium	Low	Medium	High	Yes
KEV	Medium	Low	Medium	High	Yes
The multisig voting	Medium	High	Low	Low	Not
Holographic consensus	High	High	High	Medium	Yes
Conviction voting	Low	Medium	Medium	High	Not
Rage quitting voting	Low	High	Medium	Medium	Not

Source: Ding *et al.* (2023).

they do not stick to the pre-defined rules outlined by the DAO. Several DAOs today use conviction voting in combination with other forms of voting described above.

(8) **Rage quitting**: This means that holders of governance tokens in a DAO can sell their entire share of tokens if they are not satisfied with the outcome of a particular vote. Rage quitting allows for the drastic expression of frustration with voting outcomes. We question if rage quitting is sustainable for the DAO. It may add risks to the operation if large token holders have the option to rage quit. Additionally, implementing such rage quitting vote functionality is complicated, as the sale of governance tokens would have to be automated by connecting the voting mechanism to an exchange (Table 3.1).

3.4 Proposal execution

In this section, we discuss the two categories of execution: automatic execution and manual execution. Automatic execution requires the proposer to submit the to-be-executed smart contract code with her proposal, and the governance platform supports automatic execution. Upon passing a proposal, the source code is automatically deployed on the blockchain and immediately live. For example, a grant proposal could be automatically executed by a simple smart contract that has one function only: to wire the proposed amount from the DAO's treasury wallet to the proposer's wallet. In the community of decentralization purists, automatic execution is preferred over manual execution as manual execution always requires an intermediary to perform a step and hence is perceived as riskier as the intermediary could be rogue. Sometimes, manual execution is unfortunately unavoidable. DAO communities may require manual execution for proposal implementations that do not natively live on a blockchain. For example, a DAO votes to set up a legal entity in a specific jurisdiction to employ local staff to work on a project off-chain. This process requires submitting paper forms to a government entity and hiring lawyers. Also, the local staff may want to be compensated in fiat money. This type of friction at the edges of on-chain and off-chain collaboration is expected. Over time, workable innovations will reduce these sources of friction. Disputes also can arise due to the challenges present at the edge of on-chain and off-chain worlds. We discuss dispute resolution in more detail in the following section.

3.5 Dispute resolution

Borrowing from Ding *et al.* (2023), we highlight the possible scenarios where disputes can emerge and factors DAO members should consider when deciding on how to resolve disputes. Then we discuss several dispute resolution methods and highlight what has become known as decentralized dispute resolution systems (DDRS).

First, disputes can arise from vulnerable smart contract source code. For example, in 2022, a rogue actor took advantage of a loophole in the Mango platform's smart contract to steal ca. USD 116 million.[4] Negligence is another reason for disputes to arise: Some

---

[4] *Source*: https://www.justice.gov/opa/pr/man-convicted-110m-cryptocurrency-scheme#:~:text=According%20to%20court%20documents%20and,of%20certain%20%20perpetual%20futures%20contracts (accessed on 7 June 2024).

DAO members do not carefully inspect the source code or do not have the capabilities to check it before using it. Ideally, everyone engaging with a smart contract would do thorough due diligence before interacting with it. If all users follow this protocol, it would remove much of the potential for disputes since everyone knows what the expected outcome is before the related transaction gets irreversibly and instantly settled on the blockchain. Other sources of contention include changes to the meta-governance parameters of a DAO that violate the constitution of a DAO and disagreements resulting from oracles feeding contentious information to blockchains.

When DAO members decide on which dispute resolution mechanism to use, they must consider the cost of the mechanism, the timeliness of the dispute resolution process and whether it is appropriate for the degree of disagreement. Ideally, the mechanism must enforce dispute resolution outcomes on-chain. But, since some disputes might extend to the off-chain realm, the mechanism must also enable a form of identification of conflicted DAO members. Currently, this can only be achieved through regular KYC methods.

Next, we provide an overview of the possible dispute resolution mechanisms: Courts, Tribunals, Industry Schemes, Mediation, Arbitration and Online Dispute Resolution (ODR). Table 3.2 compares these mechanisms across various characteristics, for example, cost, efficiency as discussed above, but also international applicability, DAO expertise and how compatible the solution is with the blockchain-native features, for instance, that identities may be largely unknown.

Decentralized dispute resolution services come in two types: single- and multi-layer. Single-layer DDRS, such as Kleros and Aragon Court, use crowdsourcing, where knowledgeable jurors stake tokens and are paid when they vote with the majority. Kleros allows appeals but with sharply increasing costs, while Aragon Court allows DAO members to submit arbitration agreements before voting on potentially contentious proposals.

Table 3.2. Dispute resolution methods.

Dispute resolution method	Cost	Efficiency	International applicability	DAO professional knowledge	Anonymous member compatibility	DAO readiness
Courts	High	Low	No	Limited	No	No
Tribunals	Low	High	No	Limited	No	No
Industry schemes	Low	High	No	Limited	No	No
Mediation	High	High	Yes	Limited	No	No
Arbitration	High	Low	Yes	Limited	No	No
Online Dispute Resolution (ODR)	Low	High	Yes	Limited	No	No

Source: Ding *et al.* (2023).

Multi-layer DDRS mechanisms, such as Jur and Juris, offer different layers for dispute resolution based on the dispute's value.[5] Jur provides the Court Layer for high-value disputes, the Open Layer for small-value disputes, and the Community Layer for medium-value disputes. Juris requires the inclusion of its arbitration code in the smart contract, and it can freeze the contract once a dispute arises. These mechanisms aim to provide decentralized and flexible alternatives to traditional legal systems for resolving on-chain and smart contract disputes.

After the discussion of DAO governance, we now move to Part 2 of the book. The following two chapters present the tools needed to analyze DAOs and make informed decisions regarding onboarding and collaboration. Chapter 4 introduces a comprehensive framework for deciphering DAOs based on their unique characteristics and functionalities. This framework will serve as a foundation for understanding the diverse landscape of DAOs by using categories,

---

[5]*Source*: https://jur.io and https://juris-marketing.netlify.app (accessed on 15 May 2024).

sub-categories and features that differentiate them. Chapter 5 delves into the risks associated with engaging with DAOs, drawing upon the six risk categories. We will propose a systematic methodology for assessing these risks, enabling financial services firms to evaluate potential partnerships with DAOs in a structured and rigorous manner. In combination, the two chapters propose a robust toolkit to navigate the complexities of the DAO ecosystem and make decisions that align with a regulated financial services firm's risk appetite and business objectives. Chapter 6 uses the two case studies to demonstrate how to use our risk assessment methodology.

References

Ding, Q., Liebau, D., Wang, W., and Xu, W., 2023. A Survey on Decentralized Autonomous Organizations (DAOs) and Their Governance. *World Scientific Annual Review of Fintech*. https://www.worldscientific.com/doi/epdf/10.1142/S281100482350001X.

Fritsch, R., Muller, M., and Wattenhofer, R., 2022. Analyzing Voting Power in Decentralized Governance: Who Controls DAOs? *Working Paper*. https://arxiv.org/abs/2204.01176.

Gompers, P., Ishii, J., Metrick, A., 2003. Corporate Governance and Equity Prices. *Quarterly Journal of Economics*. https://www.jstor.org/stable/25053900.

Lalley, S. and Weyl, E., 2012. Quadratic Voting: How Mechanism Design Can Radicalize Democracy. *American Economic Association Papers and Proceedings*. https://papers.ssrn.com/sol3/papers.cfm?abstract_id=2003531.

Nenova, T., 2003. The Value of Corporate Voting Rights and Control: A Cross-country Analysis. *Journal of Financial Economics*. https://doi.org/10.1016/S0304-405X(03)00069-2.

Tan, J., Merk, T., Hubbard, S., Oak, E., Pirovich, J., Rennie, E., Hoefer, R., Zargham, M., Potts, J., Berg, C., Youngblom, R., De Filippi, P., Frey, S., Strnad, J., Mannan, M., Nabben, K., Elrrifai, S., Hartnell, J., Hill, B., Maddox, A., Lim, W., South, T., Juels. A., and Boneh, D., 2023. Open Problems in DAOs. *Working Paper*. https://arxiv.org/abs/2310.19201.

Yermack, D., 2010. Shareholder Voting and Corporate Governance. *Annual Review of Financial Economics*. https://www.annualreviews.org/doi/abs/10.1146/annurev-financial-073009-104034.

PART 2

Chapter 4

How to Decipher a DAO

Abstract

This chapter presents a comprehensive framework for understanding the diverse landscape of decentralized autonomous organizations (DAOs). We organize the framework into seven main categories: objectives, community, governance, economics, finance, technology, and legal and regulatory. Each category is further divided into sub-categories and features, allowing for a detailed analysis of a DAO's characteristics. The chapter explores the various objectives that drive DAO creation, the composition and roles within DAO communities, the governance processes and structures, the economic incentives and treasury management, the underlying blockchain technology and software, and the legal and regulatory considerations.

As of May 2024, DeepDAO, an analytics site for DAOs, is tracking nearly 2400 DAOs that manage USD 20 billion collectively. There is currently no standard way of categorizing DAOs. DeepDAO splits them into 14 categories.[1] These categories are not exclusive. For example, in DeepDAO, SuperRare appears in both art and culture and non-fungible token (NFT) categories. Ding *et al.* (2023) use a similar categorical approach.[2] There is ongoing research to improve

---

[1]https://deepdao.io/organizations (accessed on 23 August 2023).

[2]Categories include collector, grant, media, protocol, philanthropy, protocol, venture, and social.

and refine the taxonomy of DAOs. Ziegler and Welpe (2022) identify DAO types that offer products and services, which are differentiated by their focus on investment, community, or networking, and further refine their taxonomy based on the characteristics of treasury, governance, and community. Peña-Calvin *et al.* (2023) categorize DAOs based on their operational domain, purpose, scope, voting process, and token usage.

Learning how to categorize the different types of DAOs and their features is an important part of the evaluation process. We draw on existing literature and introduce elements that we consider most useful for financial services professionals. Our framework is organized as follows — at the top level, there are seven categories: objectives, community, governance, economics, finance, technology, and legal and regulatory. Below each of these categories are sub-categories and their features. Given the fluid and dynamic nature of DAOs, it is important to note that a DAO can possess one or more features within each category. Table 4.1 helps deepen the understanding of DAO features and can be used as a guide to collect standard material data about DAOs.

4.1 Objectives

Individuals and groups create DAOs to virtually congregate, organize themselves, and work on objectives. These objectives can be as varied as raising money for investment or collaborating for research. Some objectives can be specific and others *ad hoc*.[3] For example, ConstitutionDAO was formed in November 2021 to buy the original copy of the US Constitution. ConstitutionDAO lost at the Soethby's auction and disbanded after that. A DAO could have started with one goal, such as investing in a specific project and then over time, evolve and expand its objectives. For example, CityDAO was started on 2 July 2021 with a single objective: to buy and tokenize land in Wyoming. It achieved this objective after registering as a Limited

---

[3]https://www.weforum.org/whitepapers/decentralized-autonomous-organizations-beyond-the-hype (accessed on 23 August 2023).

Table 4.1. DAO framework.

Categories		Sub-categories	Features				
Categories	Objectives	Invest in profit	Venture DAOs	Collector DAOs			
		Invest in public goods	Impact DAOs	Grant DAOs			
		Build products & services	Protocol DAOs	Decentralized apps DAOs			
		Networking & collaboration	Social DAOs				
	Community	Membership	Token ownership				
		Membership identification	Anonymous	Pseudonymous	Named		
		Membership roles	Founders	Delegates	Multisig key holders	Contributors	Ordinary members
		Remuneration	Governance tokens	Other tokens			
	Governance	Process	Off-chain and on-chain voting	Automatic or multi-sig execution	Voting models		
		Structure	Council and committees	SubDAOs			
		Dispute resolution	Physical world institutions	Online	Decentralized dispute resolution		

(*Continued*)

Table 4.1. (*Continued*)

Categories		Sub-categories			Features	
Categories	**Economics**	Governance token	Voting	Staking		
		Reputation	Reputation score	Non-transferable token		
	Finance	Funding	Private Sale	ICO	Airdrop	
		Treasury	Activities	Size	Diversification	
	Technology	Blockchain platform	Transaction fees	Scalability	Stability	Privacy
		DAO software	Smart contract templates	DAO-as-a-service		
	Legal & Regulatory	Legal wrapper	Yes	No		
		Type of legal wrappers	Limited liability company/ partnership	Foundation	DAO-specific legal entity	
		Associated legal entities	Yes - what others	No		

Liability Company (LLC) in Wyoming and raising sufficient funds to make the purchase.[4] Since then, the DAO's objectives have expanded as it continued to give grants to build on-chain community-governed cities and to buy land in other parts of the US and the world. In this regard, DAOs are similar to companies that adapt their businesses to the changing environment. However, at any point in time, a DAO will have a predominant goal and activity. We will focus on four sub-categories: invest in profit, invest in public goods, build products and services, and networking and collaboration.

4.1.1 *Invest for profit*

DAOs that pursue investment for profit are typically called Venture and Collector DAOs. They raise funds to invest in blockchains and Web3-related projects. Currently, one of the largest Investment DAOs on the DeepDAO platform with a treasury size of over USD 3 billion is BitDAO.[5] BitDAO's early investors in 2021 include Brevan Howard, Pantera, Peter Thiel, and Jump Capital.[6] In May 2023, BitDAO merged with Mantle, and the new entity was rebranded as Mantle.[7] Mantle's USD 200 million venture fund is currently investing in applications and builders within the Mantle ecosystem.[8] Another Investment DAO called The LAO was set up in 2020.[9] The LAO invests in Ethereum-related projects in infrastructure, decentralized finance (DeFi), NFTs, gaming, and other DAOs. A third example is MetaCartel Ventures DAO which invests in early-stage decentralized applications.[10]

Collector DAOs invest in art and collectibles. They are often set up with the objective of collecting NFTs. Currently, the two main

---

[4]https://daotimes.com/the-story-of-citydao-explain-through-timeline (accessed on 22 August 2023).
[5]https://docs.bitdao.io (accessed on 24 August 2023).
[6]https://app.dealroom.co/companies/bitdao (accessed on 12 September 2023).
[7]https://thedefiant.io/bitdao-approves-rebrand-and-token-swap (accessed on 12 September 2023).
[8]https://www.mantle.xyz/ecofund (accessed on 12 September 2023).
[9]https://thelao.io (accessed on 24 August 2023).
[10]https://metacartel.xyz (accessed on 24 August 2023).

types of high-value NFTs that Collector DAOs are interested in are art NFTs and profile picture (PFP) NFTs. PFP NFTs are often used as profile pictures of their owners on social media platforms. Typically, PFP NFTs are a collection of randomly generated and unique images of punks, apes, cats, and dogs. The NFT craze of 2021 spawned thousands of PFP NFT collections of which some, for example, CryptoPunks and Bored Ape Yacht Club, have become high-status digital assets.[11,12] An example of a Collector DAO is Flamingo DAO which was launched in October 2020. Its portfolio consists of art and PFP NFTs, including CryptoPunks, Chrome Squiggles, Ringers by Dmitri Cherniak, and Autoglyphs.[13]

4.1.2   *Invest in public goods*

DAOs that invest in public goods are known as Impact DAOs and Grant DAOs. In terms of treasury size, Impact and Grant DAOs may not be as large as Venture DAOs, but their ambitions are huge and tend to tackle more "wicked problems," which are difficult, complex, and require a significant change of mindsets and behavior. The general aim of Impact DAOs is to produce a positive social impact. Focus areas include environmental sustainability and the creation and maintenance of digital public goods, for example, Gitcoin DAO funds projects that are focused on open-source software, climate solutions and to date has distributed over USD 50 million in grants to nearly 4000 projects.[14,15] KlimaDAO is aiming to incentivize demand for carbon credits by using blockchains to bring transparency to the current inefficient and opaque carbon trading system.

4.1.3   *Build products and services*

In this category, there are Protocol DAOs, decentralized apps (DApps) DAOs, and DAO tooling. We define Protocol DAOs as those

---

[11]https://www.larvalabs.com/cryptopunks (accessed on 24 August 2023).
[12]https://boredapeyachtclub.com/# (accessed on 24 August 2023).
[13]https://flamingodao.xyz/collection (accessed on 11 August 2023).
[14]https://grants.gitcoin.co (accessed on 12 September 2023).
[15]https://impact.gitcoin.co (accessed on 12 September 2023).

governing Layer 1 (L1) and Layer 2 (L2) blockchain networks, such as Ethereum and Arbitrum, respectively. A Layer 1 is the foundational infrastructure on which DApps are built. Layer 1 blockchains validate and finalize transactions. Improving scalability on Layer 1 networks can be challenging, hence developers created Layer 2 networks. L2s are built on top of L1s to improve scalability, speed, and cost-effectiveness, but rely on L1s for security and consensus. At the time of our writing, the Layer 2 concept is still in its infancy. For example, a specific type of Layer 2, based on what is known as an optimistic rollup, can take up to 7 days to sync back to the Ethereum blockchain. Another Layer 2 approach is the ZK-rollup, which appears to be highly promising as it brings down the time to sync back to Layer 1 to just minutes. Examples of DApps DAOs include Uniswap, Aave, Curve, and Maker.

4.1.4 *Networking and collaboration*

Social DAOs' main objective is to bring people with shared interests and values together both online and in the physical world. Friends with Benefits (FWB) DAO is a social collective of creatives and builders from the crypto and cultural fields who meet online and in person to network and collaborate.[16] LexDAO is a non-profit association of legal professionals whose objective is to incorporate blockchains and codes into the legal system. To achieve this aim, membership in the LexDAO offers education, referrals for work, and project collaboration.

The DAO categories presented in this section are by no means exhaustive. DAOs are still in the early stages of experimentation. As these organizations continue to expand and evolve, new categories will emerge.

4.2 Community

The community category addresses the people element of DAOs. How do individuals join a DAO? What information do they need to

---

[16]https://www.fwb.help (accessed on 13 September 2023).

reveal about themselves for membership? What types of membership roles are available and how are they incentivized? To tackle these questions, we look at the sub-categories of membership, membership identification, membership roles, and remuneration.

4.2.1 *Membership*

Individuals interested in interacting with a DAO can start off first by joining the DAO's social media platforms. Most DAOs allow open access to online discussions on their social media platforms including Discord and X. This access gives curious visitors an opportunity to get to know the DAO and their members before deciding whether to commit further. However, to be a member of the DAO and participate in its activities, such as voting, would usually require ownership of governance tokens. There are three ways to obtain tokens: direct purchase, airdrops, or reward for work contributed to the DAO. The tokens of mature DAOs are freely traded on centralized exchanges like Coinbase, whereas tokens of newer DAOs are available on decentralized exchanges (DEX) like Uniswap. An example of an airdrop was the launch of ApeCoin. The ApeCoin token was distributed to owners of the popular NFT projects Bored Ape Yacht Club and Mutant Ape Yacht Club, their creators Yuga Labs, and other investors. After the initial distribution, ApeCoin was free to trade on crypto exchanges. As long as one owns ApeCoin, one is considered a member of ApeCoin DAO. Some DAOs allow individuals to do work to earn their tokens. Being able to earn membership through effort and sponsorship gives people without the financial means to buy tokens a fairer chance to participate. For example, the VeBetterDAO ecosystem rewards users with its B3TR token when they carry out sustainability-related activities like picking up garbage.

4.2.2 *Membership identification*

On the internet, there are three common types of identity: anonymous, pseudonymous, and named. Anonymous means a person cannot be identified in any way by their physical world identity. In this book, we refer to physical world identities as those documented by passports and other government-issued identity proofs. Pseudonymous means a person's physical world identity is not revealed, but their actions and words are revealed online, including their public blockchain wallet addresses. Named means a person's physical world identity is known. Currently, only a minority of DAOs require their members' identities to be known. These are typically Investment DAOs that want to comply with Know Your Client (KYC) standards. For example, to apply to become a member of Flamingo DAO, a new member must provide documentation to satisfy anti-money laundering (AML), KYC requirements, and compliance with sanction regulations. They also need to prove their accredited investor status under US law.[17] Outside of select Investment DAOs, most DAOs do not require members to reveal their physical world identities and thus many members remain anonymous or pseudonymous.

The issue of DAO membership identity is complex and evolving, with technical, regulatory, and philosophical challenges. Privacy is the core tenet of blockchain philosophy. But when DAOs interact with the off-chain world, including financial institutions, the latter demand identity information. Hence, striking a balance between privacy and accountability is an ongoing issue for DAOs, a topic which will be explored in Chapters 5 and 8.

4.2.3 *Membership roles*

Although a DAO is structurally flat, there are still a variety of roles and responsibilities. The following are the common types of membership roles: founders, delegates, multi-signature key holders, contributors, and ordinary members.

Founders create DAOs. Like most startups, DAOs come to life when an individual or group is motivated to start a project or

---

[17]https://docs.flamingodao.xyz/Membership.html#how-can-i-contribute-to-flamingo-and-become-a-member (accessed on 19 September 2023).

organization to achieve an objective. They then rally others to join them in their mission and find resources to build. Founders in traditional startups are able to set up legal entities, whereas DAO founders navigate in more uncertain legal and regulatory environments.

Delegates are representatives of other token holders: delegators. Delegates propose and vote on behalf of the delegators. Typically, the aspiring delegate pitches to other members to be chosen as their representative. They would put their profiles online detailing their reasons for running, relevant skills and experiences, and previous contributions. Based on this information, members will choose who they want to delegate their voting rights to. Voting rights can be delegated and revoked anytime by signing a transaction on the blockchain.

Multi-signature key holders control multi-sig wallets and multi-sig smart contracts. In a multi-sig setup, multiple digital signatures are required for approval. Control is split between several individual key holders. For example, if a multi-sig is set up as "2 of 3," then 2 of the 3 pre-approved key holders need to sign. This setup is known as an "M of N" requirement where N is the total number of approved key holders and M is the number that must approve and sign before an action is taken. Once DAO members have voted on a proposal, the multi-sig key holders still need to approve its implementation. Using the multi-sig concept carries a risk: Multi-sig key holders can do nothing or implement something incompatible with the proposal. DAOs use the multi-sig concept to control their treasury wallet and approve important code changes. Multi-sig key holders have immense power, hence knowing how they are selected is a critical aspect of understanding a DAO's governance. Multi-sig key holders are selected in different ways. For a DAO that is new, small, and young, it is not unusual for the multi-sig key holders to be part of the founding team and self-appointed. For DAOs with stricter and higher governance standards, some of the common methods are voting by DAO members and random selection to avoid bias. Due to the risk outlined above, some DAOs choose not to use the multi-sig concept at all.

Contributors in DAOs are developers, administrators, and facilitators. Developers are responsible for the technical development and maintenance of the DAO's blockchain, smart contracts, and software. Administrators and facilitators manage activities, such as proposal curation, organizing voting periods, and maintaining internal and external communication on the DAO's social media channels.

Ordinary members are the largest category of DAO participants. As part of the DAO's governance process, they participate in discussions, put forward proposals, delegate their voting power to delegates, or vote themselves.

Although we have described the main membership roles in DAOs, it is important to remember that DAO roles are not as clear-cut and fixed as positions in traditional organizations. It is possible for an individual to carry out responsibilities that overlap different roles.

Business-to-DAO (B2DAO) companies are not part of DAOs, but they offer tools and services that include treasury management and accounting, community management, discovery and analytics, governance and voting, and human resources management. The B2DAO concept offers business potential for financial services firms that consider DAOs as possible clients in asset management, insurance, custody, and other financial activities. Although DAOs started in investing in digital assets, increasingly, some DAOs are expanding into traditional assets.

4.2.4 *Remuneration*

Working in a DAO is unlike working for a company with clear employment contracts and scope of work. DAO work offers a hybrid of ownership, freelancing, volunteering, and employment in different proportions. In "Work for Decentralized Autonomous Organisation," Ilyushina (2023) tracks a typical lifecycle of a DAO worker. The first step is to join the DAO's social media platform, often Discord. Next, the worker must start getting noticed by the existing DAO members. For example, the worker helps interested parties by answering queries about the DAO. They could also put forward useful proposals to improve the DAO. The purpose of participating and doing work is to build a reputation within the DAO. The work done at this stage may or may not be remunerated. Remuneration is in digital form, in governance tokens, or in other tokens, such as BTC, ETH, or stablecoins. Not all work is paid. If the mission of the DAO resonates strongly with a worker, they may be motivated to contribute without regular pay.

DAO labor is not well researched at the time of our writing and data sources are sparse. DeepDAO shows 7.6 million governance token holders, but we do not know how many are paid workers.[18] Gitcoin and Bankless DAO surveyed 422 members from 230 DAOs. Despite the small sample size, the survey offered interesting insights. Eighty percent of the participants were male and aged 20–40, living in over 290 distinct cities across the world. As DAOs become more common and represent a viable source of work for more people, DAO members in turn become potentially attractive clients for financial services firms. These DAO members could be retail customers, high net-worth clients, or entrepreneurs looking to start a relationship with financial services companies for their businesses.

4.3   Governance

Previously in Chapter 3, we explain what DAO governance entails and introduce the concepts of agenda setting, voting, execution, and dispute resolution. This section uses the different types of governance features in process, structure, and dispute resolution to decipher DAOs.

4.3.1   *Process*

Voting plays a significant role in a DAO's decision-making process. DAO members vote off-chain and on-chain. In off-chain voting,

---

[18]https://deepdao.io/organizations (accessed on 26 September 2023).

individual votes are not stored on the blockchain, but the final result is. An example of a popular platform for this voting system is Snapshot.[19] With Snapshot, DAO members sign their vote using their wallets, but these signed messages are stored with Snapshot and hence do not incur gas fees.[20] When all votes are in, the result is stored on the InterPlanetary File System (IPFS) and hashed on the blockchain. The cost of a single transaction on a blockchain is much lower compared to each voter paying gas fees for their individual vote. When voting occurs on-chain, each individual vote incurs a transaction fee. Votes that are captured on public blockchains are transparent and immutable. Tally is a front end that facilitates this process.[21]

Some prominent DAOs use a hybrid approach, combining off-chain and on-chain elements in their voting process. Examples are dYdX and Uniswap.[22,23] A hybrid approach offers the best of both worlds: gasless voting in the early stages of the process and the subsequent immutable recording of end results on a blockchain.

The proposal, once approved, is executed automatically by smart contracts, or by multisig key holders. For automatic execution of approved proposals, implementation by smart contracts on a blockchain is transparent, immutable, and easily verifiable. This approach works for any proposal that can be implemented by a smart contract. Examples include token transfers and protocol updates. Although we are sympathetic to the decentralization ethos, we would argue that at this stage, it is not possible for all proposals to be automatically executed by smart contracts. There is still a need for

---

[19]https://snapshot.org/# (accessed on 8 January 2024).

[20]https://ethereum.stackexchange.com/questions/38395/gas-requirement-for-ethereum-message-signing (accessed on 17 May 2024).

[21]https://docs.tally.xyz/knowledge-base/proposals/voting-on-proposals (accessed on 8 February 2024).

[22]https://www.dydxdao.info/dydx-governance/proposal-lifecycle (accessed on 9 January 2024).

[23]https://uniswap.org/governance (accessed on 9 January 2024).

some degree of human intervention. This includes legal agreements and investing in traditional off-chain assets. Ziegler and Weiple (2022) found that only 13% of DAOs use automatic execution.

In Chapter 3, we covered the extensive range of voting models available to a DAO: quorum, quadratic, reputation-based, knowledge-extractable, holographic consensus, conviction, and rage quitting. The choice of voting model reveals key insights about the DAO's governance philosophy and power dynamics. For instance, if the DAO uses quadratic voting, it is a signal that it is attempting to mitigate the outsized influence of whales and allowing smaller token holders to influence decisions. However, if the DAO uses voting models based on reputation and knowledge, versus purely based on token holdings, it could help encourage more active participation from the community.

4.3.2 *Structure*

Most DAOs operate on a relatively flat structure. However, there are some that have councils and committees. In the 150 DAOs examined by Appel and Grennan (2023), 33% had "appointed representatives or board-like councils." These councils can have influence over the proposal process and some even have veto powers. For example, the Polkadot Council has the power to veto dangerous or malicious proposals.[24] Another example of a DAO with Governing Councils is Synthetix, a derivatives liquidity protocol for DeFi. The Synthetix protocol is governed by four councils. The Spartan Council votes in Improvement Proposals pertaining to the Synthetix protocol. The Treasury Council manages the treasury and pays for the cost of growing the protocol including remuneration to the contributors. The Grants Council decides on which grants and bounties to fund. The fourth and last Council is the Ambassador Council, which is responsible for promoting Synthetix in the DeFi ecosystem via

---

[24]https://wiki.polkadot.network/docs/maintain/maintain-guides-how-to-join-council (accessed on 7 October 2024).

partnerships and seeking governance power in protocols that are beneficial to Synthetix.[25,26]

SubDAOs are sometimes created by parent DAOs to distribute responsibilities. SubDAOs are tied to the parent's mission but can have their own on-chain governance and even legal entities. dYdX is a DEX for trading perpetual futures contracts for cryptocurrencies and is governed by dYdX DAO.[27] The parent DAO created a SubDAO for Operations. The Operations SubDAO has a governing legal entity which is the dYdX Operational Trust formed under Guernsey law.[28] In another example, the SubDAOs of Nouns DAO are created spontaneously by individuals who are inspired by the parent DAO.[29] Nouns DAO auctions unique, algorithmically generated NFTs called "Nouns" daily and uses the auction proceeds to fund community-driven projects and initiatives. The SubDAOs then create NFTs that are derivatives of Nouns NFTs to expand the Nouns ecosystem. Generally, SubDAOs have a degree of autonomy in their decision-making and operations while still aligning with the overall mission and values of the parent DAO. This autonomy can be motivating for members and allows for more agile decision-making within the perimeter of the SubDAO.

We conclude this section on DAO structure with some food for thought. If DAOs are successful and grow bigger in membership size in the future, is it possible to stay completely free of hierarchy as per the idealized, flat version of a DAO? Or should we take heed from history? As Durrant and Durrant (1968) state in *The Lessons of History*, "most governments have been oligarchies — ruled by a minority, chosen either by birth, as in aristocracies, or by a religious organization, as in theocracies, or by wealth, as in democracies. It is unnatural (...) for a majority to rule, for a majority can seldom be

---

[25] https://synthetix.io/governance (accessed on 11 April 2024).

[26] This video shows how Synthetix evolved to a council governance structure. *Source:* https://www.youtube.com/watch?v=K2fGO9FSvQk (accessed on 17 May 2024).

[27] https://www.dydxdao.info (accessed on 11 April 2024).

[28] https://www.dydxopsdao.com/about (accessed on 11 April 2024).

[29] https://nouns.center/subdaos (accessed on 3 June 2024).

organized for united and specific action, and a minority can. If most abilities is contained in a minority of men, minority government is as inevitable as the concentration of wealth; the majority can do no more than periodically throw out one minority and set up another." As we shall see in the following section, research shows that freely traded governance tokens can have a centralizing effect unless it is mitigated by design or regulation.

4.3.3 *Dispute resolution*

The effectiveness and legitimacy of a DAO's governance system depend, in part, on its ability to handle disputes fairly and efficiently. When members of a DAO disagree on a particular decision or course of action, the dispute resolution mechanism helps the parties come to an agreement and maintain the integrity of the organization.

The choice of dispute resolution method is a significant aspect of a DAO's governance design. As covered in detail in Section 3.5, there is a range of possible dispute resolution mechanisms: courts, tribunals, industry schemes, mediation, arbitration in the physical world, and online dispute resolution (ODR). For DAOs, blockchain-enabled decentralized dispute resolution services are often used.

4.4 Economics

We can use economics to understand DAOs in a few ways. One way is via an emergent field popularly known as Tokenomics which studies the design and monetary policy of a crypto token for a blockchain ecosystem. Tokenomics often uses principles from game theory to create incentives and outcomes. Later in this section, we touch on how DAOs use tokens as incentives.

A second way is to investigate DAOs as a new kind of institution. What is an "institution" in this context? In New Institutional Economics (NIE), a field that gained prominence from the 1960s with the work of Nobel Prize economists Ronald Coase, Oliver Williamson, and Douglass North, institutions refer to formal and informal structures that govern economies, as well as social and political interaction. Formal structures include laws and property rights, whereas informal ones refer to customs and traditions (North, 1991). Prior to NIE, economic theory used price as the standard unit to understand market transactions. In contrast, NIE uses transaction costs to explain how such costs influence the type of economic activities and structure of institutions that emerge. Transaction costs include search and information costs to evaluate potential partners; bargaining, monitoring, and enforcement (Lumineau *et al.*, 2021); asset specificity (investments that are highly specialized for a particular transaction but have little alternative use); and opportunism (self-interested behavior of individuals to deceive or mislead) (Williamson, 1985).

Building on the ideas of NIE, Davidson *et al.* (2018) coined the term "Institutional Cryptoeconomics" to argue that blockchain (and by extension blockchain-based DAO) is a "new institutional technology for economic coordination." Institutional Cryptoeconomics examines "how blockchains interact with our existing and future social institutions, from the nature of contracts, to the shape of the firm, to the structures of global trade..." (Berg *et al.*, 2019). How should we assess blockchain-based DAOs through transaction cost theory? Theoretically, given how DAOs help mitigate agency costs (as explored in Section 1.3 of Chapter 1), monitoring and enforcement costs of blockchain-based DAOs should be lower. However, as Lumineau *et al.* (2021) argue, the design costs associated with anticipating many possible scenarios and codifying them into smart contracts on a blockchain would be high. Hence, if a DAO relies on a high proportion of its processes to be carried out by smart contracts, then it will spend more resources in the design process. When a financial services professional is assessing the viability of a DAO's economic activities, it is useful to apply transaction cost theory to question whether a DAO is a more or less competitive institution to carry out the activity in question versus a traditional firm or government. If a DAO can demonstrably show that its overall transaction costs are lower than a firm, then there is more ground for the DAO to compete and succeed.

4.4.1 *Governance tokens*

In economics, incentives play an important role in understanding human behavior. We instinctively respond to incentives because we are motivated by self-interest, status, and a desire to fit in with social groups and cultural norms. Incentives are used to appeal to our extrinsic motivation of attaining external goals of success, recognition, wealth, and power.

In a traditional firm, incentives for employees are job promotions and financial rewards. In contrast, compensation for DAO community members is not always clear and guaranteed for their contributions. As such, we need to dig into what incentives motivate individuals to participate in DAOs. We look at the two most common tools to incentivize behavior in blockchain-based DAOs: governance tokens and reputation.

Governance tokens confer voting rights. As such, members who desire to have a say in the DAO's decision-making will be motivated to own these tokens. Accumulating governance tokens is a means to power and to wield influence in a DAO. Given the decentralized ideal of DAOs, there is a natural suspicion of any group that becomes too powerful and plutocratic.

In a 2023 paper by Bakos and Halaburda titled "Will Blockchains Disintermediate Platforms? Limits to Credible Decentralization in DAOs," the authors show that a DAO with freely traded governance tokens has a strong tendency toward centralization of control, and hence limits the degree of decentralization. Such concentration can be mitigated by design or regulation, though enforcement would be challenging. As such, even in a DAO striving for decentralization, the paper argues that in the presence of freely traded governance tokens, DAOs would give rise to a "new class of intermediaries."

However, it can be argued that the existence of a powerful entity in itself is not necessarily negative for a DAO. Instead, it depends on how this entity chooses to vote. If it votes in alignment with the DAO's interest, then it can be considered benign. On the contrary, governance tokens can be used in hostile takeovers whereby an entity acquires sufficient governance tokens to seize control over the DAO's decision-making process and force outcomes that are detrimental to the members. In 2022, a DeFi project called Beanstalk lost USD 182 million after an attacker bought a controlling stake of tokens and voted to send all the funds to themselves.[30] In 2023, a bad actor put forth a malicious proposal in Tornado Cash DAO that hid a secret code that granted the attacker the power of majority rule.[31]

It is important to note that the utility of these tokens resides in their governance features. However, participants in the current nascent crypto market buy them to speculate and for potential capital appreciation.

Lastly, governance tokens can also be staked to earn rewards. Staking means locking the tokens on a blockchain network to contribute to its security. In return for locking the tokens, the DAO will earn rewards in the form of additional tokens.

4.4.2 *Reputation*

"Reputations will be of central importance, far more important in dealings than even the credit ratings of today," according to Timothy May, Co-Founder of the Cypherpunk movement.[32] Our individual reputation is a form of social capital that has implications for our actions and effectiveness in any group setting. Reputations can be known and transmitted through word of mouth, or more formally recorded and shared with a wide audience, for example, seller ratings on digital marketplaces and reviews of restaurants on popular review sites. Similarly, reputation in DAOs matters too. Whereas a good rating as a seller on eBay begets more sales, what advantages accrue to a good reputation in a DAO? In a DAO, community membership roles are fluid: a member could be making a proposal, running to be a delegate, or be in a leadership position (if the DAO has Councils

---

[30] https://www.coindesk.com/tech/2022/04/17/attacker-drains-182m-from-bean stalk-stablecoin-protocol (accessed on 3 February 2024).

[31] https://www.web3isgoinggreat.com/single/tornado-cash-governance-attack (accessed on 5 February 2024).

[32] https://groups.csail.mit.edu/mac/classes/6.805/articles/crypto/cypherpunks/ may-crypto-manifesto.html (accessed on 4 February 2023).

and a more hierarchical structure). Having a good reputation will help advance the member's goals in these various pursuits.

The ways that reputation is measured vary among DAOs, but some common metrics are based on the submission of well-considered proposals, voting on proposals, completing assigned tasks, and contributing to discussions and proposals on online forums. An example of reputation scoreboards is the profiles of stewards of Gitcoin DAO.[33] Each steward's profile has a quantified record of their Snapshot voting history and forum activity, and their cumulative activities are scored according to an algorithm.[34] In this case, a better reputation will help increase the steward's influence.

At this point, it is useful to introduce the concept of soulbound tokens (SBTs). SBTs were introduced in a 2022 paper by Ohlhaver *et al.* as "publicly visible, non-transferable (but possibly revocable-by-the-issuer) tokens." During the 2021 and 2022 NFTs craze, some NFTs traded at obscenely astronomical prices. The authors came up with the concept of SBTs as an antidote to the hyper-financialization and trading of NFTs. SBT's differentiating and distinguishing feature is that it cannot be transferred once it has been issued to a wallet. In using the term "soulbound," the writers were inspired by "soulbound" items on the World of Warcraft game which are permanently attached to the player upon acquisition and cannot be transferred to another player. Whereas governance tokens can be traded, SBTs cannot and thus can be used to give a more accurate representation of the entity's attributes and reputation. Since the concept was introduced in 2022, various DAOs have been experimenting with the use of SBTs as a reputation tool. Some DAOs use reputation tokens to represent a score. TRUST is an example of a reputation token used in Trusted Seed.[35,36] Members can increase their TRUST score by carrying out activities that advance the DAO's

---

[33] https://gitcoin.karmahq.xyz (accessed on 17 January 2024).

[34] https://www.gitcoin.co/blog/delegation-done-right-steward-health-cards (accessed on 17 January 2024).

[35] https://trustedseed.org/trusted-seed-a-value-driven-community-advancing-reg en-economies#d5186a236f9140e9a6033a63a9f1f2ef (accessed on 18 January 2024).

[36] https://trustedseed.org (accessed on 18 January 2024).

mission including actively helping others on their Discord channel and earning official recognition for their work.

4.5 Finance

When considering a DAO's finances, the two important subcategories are the DAO's funding process and the way its treasury is managed.

4.5.1 *Funding*

At the early stage of fundraising, a DAO will typically conduct a private sale of its token to a select group of investors. Often, these investors are angels and venture capital (VC) funds. Some examples of VC funds that are active investors in DAOs include Paradigm, Multicoin Capital, and Andreessen Horowitz. Investment and Venture DAOs are also potential investors in new DAOs at the private sale. Later in the fundraising process, the DAO could choose to carry out an initial coin sale (ICO).[37] In an ICO, the project creates and sells a new digital token in exchange for more established tokens of BTC, ETH, or stablecoins.

DAOs often use airdrops as a marketing strategy to grow their user base (Makaridis *et al.*, 2021). Airdrops are the allotment of free tokens to a pre-identified group of digital wallet addresses. Unlike ICOs and private sales, recipients of airdrops do not pay for their tokens, and the DAO does not receive any new funds from an airdrop exercise. The expectation is that this marketing strategy will lead to more individuals being interested in the DAO and purchasing additional tokens.

4.5.2 *Treasury*

DAO treasuries carry out the following potential types of activities: fund initiatives and projects or investments approved by the

---

[37]https://consensys.io/blog/how-daos-are-funded (accessed on 12 October 2023).

community, provide grants to those contributing to the DAO ecosystem, and pay for the operational expenses of the DAO. A DAO's treasury holds the collective financial assets of the DAO. Generally, these financial assets are in the form of digital assets. When assessing a DAO's treasury, size is a natural starting point to gauge how well-funded the DAO is. Some websites that report on the total value of DAO treasuries are DeepDAO and DefiLlama.[38,39] As of writing, the top four DAOs manage treasuries from USD 1 billion to nearly USD 3 billion. The size in DAO treasuries reached a peak of USD 35 billion in 2021 and shrunk to USD 12.4 billion in January 2023.[40] Since DAO treasuries hold mostly crypto tokens, and token prices are volatile, we must be vigilant that DAO treasury sizes can change significantly. Since the main source of DAO funding is the issuance of its own governance token, it therefore makes sense to question how much of the portfolio remains in the DAO's token. If a DAO has an active treasury management approach, it may choose to diversify into other assets. However, if it does not, then the portfolio will be heavily weighted in its own token and hence leads to concentration risks. Should the token price drop significantly, such an outsized exposure will be catastrophic for the DAO. On the contrary, those in charge of managing the treasury also face the potential reaction of the community. If the DAO treasury sells large amounts of its own token in its attempt to diversify, it could raise the following questions: Why is the treasury selling its own token? Have they lost faith in the project? This situation could lead to a self-fulfilling death spiral for the token price.

When discussing the size of DAO treasuries and the outsized role of governance tokens, we must highlight that there is currently

---

[38] https://defillama.com (accessed on 16 October 2023).

[39] https://deepdao.io/organizations (accessed on 16 October 2023).

[40] https://daotimes.com/the-dao-landscape-and-treasuries-a-dao-annual-report/#:~:text=Notably%2C%20the%20total%20value%20locked,winter%20and%20dwindling%20crypto%20prices (accessed on 16 October 2023).

no generally accepted accounting framework for DAOs (Lommers *et al.*, 2023). Currently, governance tokens are recorded as assets in the treasury. Whether this is a fair representation by current International Finance Reporting Standards (IFRS) is debatable, argues Schoonwinkel in his 2023 paper "Towards Fair Presentation of DAO treasuries: An Evaluation of Native Governance Token Reporting Practices." As DAOs grow in size and importance, it is increasingly imperative that an accepted and consistent framework is adopted.

4.6 Technology

DAOs exist on blockchains. As such, when we review DAOs under the category of technology, we first ask which blockchain platform the DAO is built on. As covered in Chapter 2, the choice of blockchain will influence transaction fees, security, decentralization, and privacy. In turn, these characteristics will have implications for the DAO.

4.6.1 *Blockchain platform*

Voter apathy is a problem for DAOs (Barbereau *et al.*, 2023). When voting, delegation of voting rights, and implementation of voting outcomes occur on-chain, fees have to be paid for each associated transaction. A DAO operating on a blockchain with low transaction costs can lower the friction costs of participation and thus remove a reason for voter apathy. As of writing, most DAOs use Ethereum as a blockchain platform. Ethereum's transaction fees depend on the level of activity on its network, and as such fees are unpredictable and can sometimes be prohibitively high. As such, DAOs are increasingly being built on Optimism, Arbitrum, Polygon, Solana, and BNB Chain. Optimism, Arbitrum, and Polygon are L2 blockchains built on the top of Ethereum. L2s handle and bundle transactions and then settle the final, aggregated state on the Ethereum blockchain. Through this process, L2s offer cheaper, more predictable transaction fees.

Despite being the first and most well-known smart contract platform, Ethereum has a scalability problem. Blockchain scalability refers to its capacity to handle transactions per second (TPS). If DAOs gain wider adoption, there will be an increase in the number of active members executing transactions concurrently. This will demand more scalable blockchains in the form of L2s and newer L1s which can process many more TPS than Ethereum. Since the launch of Ethereum, engineers have worked on new L1s that increase the critical TPS metric to facilitate broad adoption of their platform. Examples include Avalanche, Near, and Solana.

In Chapter 2, we highlighted the importance of a blockchain's stability, i.e. its ability to stay "live" and not suffer any outages or downtime. If a DAO is on a blockchain that is unstable, it can have adverse implications for the DAO's activities. Imagine a DeFi DAO with billions of dollars in borrowing and lending subjected to long outages. This will create uncertainty and panic, leading to market volatility and possibly trading delays and losses.

As more communities use DAOs, there will be more demand for privacy-preserving technology. Examples of privacy-preserving technology include zero-knowledge proofs, homomorphic encryption, and multiparty computation (see Chapter 2). DAOs handle sensitive information, including strategic decisions, financial transactions, and sometimes personal data of their members. DAOs in competitive industries need to keep their plans confidential to maintain an advantage. In some cases, privacy might even be in keeping with regulatory compliance, for example, the General Data Protection Regulation (GDPR) in the European Union and the Personal Data Protection Act (PDPA) in Singapore.

4.6.2 *DAO software*

DAO software are governance processes encoded in smart contracts that cover a range of DAO activities, including proposing, voting, management of tasks and funds, and dispute resolution, among others. In other words, DAO software are smart contract templates used to run a DAO on a blockchain. These templates specify rules and processes for the DAO members and are usually open source. Examples of such templates are Compound Governor and

Open Zeppelin Governor. Nestled within these templates are smart contract processes for different outcomes.

An example of one such process is the timelock. Timelock is a security feature that sets a delay before a proposal is implemented on-chain.[41] Compound, a leading DeFi protocol, uses timelock in its governance process.[42] If a majority votes for the proposal, it is queued in the timelock for 2 days. This gives the community time to thoroughly review the passed proposal one more time. If a malicious proposal was passed, the timelock window allows the community to cancel the proposal. When the timelock period expires without intervention, then the proposal is executed.

Using such smart contract templates still requires a certain level of technical expertise. Since 2016, entities such as Aragon, DAOHaus, and Colony have emerged to offer DAO-as-a-service. They enable users with no coding expertise to create DAOs easily and thus facilitate a rapid rise in new DAOs.

4.7 Legal and regulatory

So far, we have not addressed the elephant in the room: the legal and regulatory treatment of DAOs. A DAO legal wrapper refers to a legal structure that is used to incorporate a DAO within a specific jurisdiction's legal system. The purpose of a legal wrapper is to give the DAO a legal status in the traditional legal system, enabling it to enter into contracts, hold assets, and engage in activities with other traditional firms. Currently, many DAOs do not have legal wrappers. This introduces potential legal, compliance, liability, and tax risks for the DAOs and their members.[43] Since DAOs are such

---

[41] https://medium.com/@solidity101/100daysofsolidity-066-%EF%B8%8F-unlocking-the-power-of-time-exploring-timelock-contracts-in-solidity-5edf32de2e89#:~:text=TimeLocks%20play%20a%20vital%20role,any%20hasty%20or%20impulsive%20actions (accessed on 7 February 2024).

[42] https://docs.compound.finance/v2/governance (accessed on 13 February 2024).

[43] https://news.bloomberglaw.com/us-law-week/the-right-legal-wrapper-can-protect-a-dao-and-its-members (accessed on 23 October 2023).

nascent entities, many jurisdictions do not even have specific legal regimes for DAOs. This raises the question of how and whether DAOs can conform to existing legal frameworks, which are designed for easily identifiable and centralized entities that operate within a territorially defined jurisdiction. DAOs, in contrast, are decentralized blockchain-based and often global communities. Therein lies the inherent tension between the decentralized setup of DAOs and the existing legal corporate frameworks. However, if a DAO wants to enter into contractual relationships in the off-chain world, there needs to be a legal party to contract with. Besides the ability to enter into contracts, a legal entity has other rights and obligations including legally owning assets, suing and defending in its own name, and paying taxes. One of the most important legal concepts is that of limited liability. Limited liability is a legal concept protecting an individual's financial responsibility for the debts and obligations of the organization they are part of. Limited liability is designed to protect the personal assets of business owners and shareholders. If a DAO has no legal wrapper, there is a possibility that DAO members are not legally protected from unlimited liability.[44]

The legal environment for DAOs is undergoing rapid changes. We are not lawyers, so we strongly recommend consulting with legal professionals in the respective jurisdictions for legal advice. In this section, we present some of the main questions when considering the legal and regulatory dimensions of DAOs. Has the DAO used a legal wrapper? If it has, what kind of legal wrapper is it? Also, what are the DAO's associated entities and their respective responsibilities? This section should be read in tandem with our interview with Hagen Rooke, Partner at Reed Smith, in Chapter 7.

4.7.1 *Does the DAO have a legal wrapper?*

The first question to ask is whether the DAO has a legal wrapper. If the DAO has no registered legal entity, it must have alternative ways of interacting with the off-chain world. A DAO may partner

---

[44]https://legalnodes.com/article/dao-legal-structure (accessed on 24 October 2023).

with a company to conduct activities on its behalf. For example, in 2021, ConstitutionDAO was created to bid for one of the original copies of the US Constitution at a Sotheby's auction. At that time, Sotheby did not accept digital currencies and did not allow DAOs to bid directly at its auctions. Hence, ConstitutionDAO partnered with a cryptocurrency exchange to convert some of its ETH to USD, partnered with a non-profit organization to make the bid on its behalf, and formed a corporation to facilitate the transfer.[45] If a DAO does not register as a legal entity, it may still be recognized by default under the law as an unincorporated association. This occurred in the case of OokiDAO where the US Commodities Futures Trading Commission (CFTC) found OokiDAO liable as an unincorporated association.[46] In some US states, an "unincorporated association" is not a legal entity separate and distinct from the people who are part of the DAO. As such, these members do not have the protection of a limited liability company. By charging that OokiDAO is an unincorporated association, the CFTC is asserting that OokiDAO's voting members are liable for the actions of the DAO.[47]

4.7.2 *Types of legal wrappers*

If a DAO chooses to wrap itself with a legal entity, what are its options? A16z, a venture firm, created a decision tree laying out options from a mostly US-centric perspective.[48] The decision tree shows that the purpose of the DAO will often dictate the most appropriate legal structure. Options include limited liability corporation, limited cooperative association (LCA), unincorporated nonprofit association (UNA), or foreign foundation (FF).

---

[45] https://corpgov.law.harvard.edu/2022/09/17/a-primer-on-daos (accessed on 24 October 2023).

[46] https://www.cftc.gov/PressRoom/PressReleases/8590-22 (accessed on 24 October 2023).

[47] https://www.kramerlevin.com/en/perspectives-search/cftc-asserts-dao-membe rs-are-liable-for-actions-of-the-dao.html (accessed on 13 February 2024).

[48] https://a16zcrypto.com/posts/article/dao-legal-entity-how-to-pick (accessed on 24 October 2023).

Currently, most jurisdictions do not have laws to incorporate DAOs. In such jurisdictions, DAOs would need to conform to the existing legal corporate structures. The most prominent traditional legal forms are corporations, partnerships and limited liability corporations, and Foundations.[49] The specifics of formation, governance, and taxation for each of these forms vary from country to country, and hence the descriptions that follow are highly generalized. If a DAO registers as a corporation, its members become shareholders of the company. The requirements of a corporation imply that select individuals must be appointed as directors to manage the company, and there must be adherence to traditional governance and administrative processes, e.g. mandatory AGM. Generally, DAOs will not choose to be incorporated as a corporation as the legal requirements and setup do not allow them to remain decentralized.

A partnership is a structure in which members share the profits and losses of an organization. Limited liability partnerships combine the limited liability feature of the corporations with some flexibility in the membership and management structure. This flexibility has made limited liability corporations (LLCs) an option for DAOs in the US. For example, Flamingo DAO which was set up to collect NFTs is registered as a Delaware LLC.[50]

A more popular form of legal entity popular with DAOs is the Foundation. A Foundation provides a "legal shield" and protects its members from unlimited liability. In the process of setting up a Foundation, a DAO Constitution needs to be drawn up. It should include the structure of the DAO and its governance process. Reflecting these terms in the Articles of Association gives them a legally binding status.[51] Several DAOs are set up as Foundations

---

[49] https://www.weforum.org/publications/decentralized-autonomous-organizati on-toolkit (accessed on 25 October 2023).

[50] https://docs.flamingodao.xyz/organization.html (accessed on 11 April 2024).

[51] https://legalnodes.com/article/dao-foundation-functions#:~:text=All%20in% 20all%2C%20in%20the,status%20and%20legitimize%20them%3B%20and (accessed on 25 October 2023).

in Switzerland, Singapore, and the Cayman Islands.[52,53] The Swiss Foundation structure has been popular in the blockchain world since it was first used by Ethereum. DAO Suisse is an association that is actively working on making Switzerland an attractive destination for DAOs and is organized as a DAO itself.[54]

Some jurisdictions recognized the fundamental differences between DAOs and traditional companies and thus created legal frameworks designed specifically for DAOs. In the US, the states of Wyoming, Tennessee, and Vermont have created legal entity types for DAOs.[55] If a DAO registers in these states, it has a legal person and can contract with third parties and appear in court. The law also enables them to pay taxes and have limited liability for their members. The DAO-friendly law recognizes that a DAO is managed by a combination of human members and smart contracts.[56] In Wyoming, the legal framework passed in March 2024 is also known as the Decentralized Unincorporated Nonprofit Association (DUNA).[57]

4.7.3 *Associated legal entities*

In the beginning, the software developers would set up an operating company at the onshore location where the developer team is predominantly based. The team then develops the code and smart contracts for the DAO. When the code and smart contracts are first deployed, the operating company typically retains control over the smart contracts. If and when the operating company decides to create

---

[52]https://legalnodes.com/article/swiss-foundation-dao-legal-wrapper (accessed on 25 October 2023).

[53]https://legalnodes.com/article/caymanian-foundation-for-dao (accessed on 25 October 2023).

[54]https://www.daosuisse.com (accessed on 25 October 2023).

[55]https://fortune.com/crypto/2024/03/08/wyoming-dao-a16z-crypto-crypto-blockchain-ooki (accessed on 11 April 2024).

[56]https://sos.wyo.gov/Business/Docs/DAOs_FAQs.pdf (accessed on 11 April 2024).

[57]https://a16zcrypto.com/posts/article/duna-for-daos (accessed on 11 April 2024).

a DAO, they will have to decide if they want to use a legal wrapper for the DAO.

Consider the example of Uniswap. Uniswap Labs was incorporated in the US in 2018 and operates https://app.uniswap.org/.[58] Uniswap Labs is a software development company that was responsible for developing large parts of the Uniswap Protocol. Uniswap Labs employs a core development team that builds and maintains the Protocol's codebase. Uniswap Labs owns the intellectual property and branding associated with the Uniswap name, and it has the right to build commercial products and services related to the Uniswap Protocol. Uniswap Labs also owns a widely used user interface (https://app.uniswap.org) for the Uniswap Protocol.[59]

In contrast, the Uniswap Protocol is a set of smart contracts governed by Uniswap DAO. As of writing, the Uniswap DAO has no legal wrapper. The DAO uses the UNI token as a voting right. UNI tokens are held by a diverse set of token holders.[60] The rights and privileges for UNI token holders are related to the governance of the Uniswap Protocol only.

This example shows that when assessing a DAO, the financial services professional has to clarify which entity the financial institution is facing and the rights and responsibilities tied to that entity.

References

Appel, I. and Grennan, J., 2023. Decentralized Governance and Digital Asset Prices. *Working Paper*. https://papers.ssrn.com/sol3/papers.cfm?abstract_id=4367209.

Bakos, Y. and Halaburda, H., 2023. Will Blockchains Disintermediate Platforms? The Problem of Credible Decentralization in DAOs. *Working Paper*. https://papers.ssrn.com/sol3/papers.cfm?abstract_id=4221512.

Barbereau, T., Smethurst, R., Papageorgiou, Sedlmeir, J., and Fridgen, G., 2023. Decentralised Finance's Timocratic Governance: The Distribution and Exercise of Tokenised Voting Rights. *Technology in Society*. https://www.sciencedirect.com/science/article/pii/S0160791X23000568.

---

[58]https://uniswap.org/privacy-policy (accessed on 24 October 2023).

[59]https://uniswap.org/terms-of-service (accessed on 11 April 2024).

[60]https://support.uniswap.org/hc/en-us/articles/8671701219853-What-is-Uniswap- (accessed on 24 October 2023).

Berg, C., Davidson, S., and Potts, J., 2019. *Understanding the Blockchain Economy: An introduction to Institutional Cryptoeconomics. Ch 1.* https://www.elgaronline.com/display/9781788974998/chapter01.xhtml.

Davidson, S., Filippi, P., and Potts, J., 2018. Blockchains and the Economic Institutions of Capitalism. *Journal of Institutional Economics.* https://www.cambridge.org/core/journals/journal-of-institutional-econom ics/article/abs/blockchains-and-the-economic-institutions-of-capitalism/ 7DFE353FEB8FA25559E6C09FE77E8291.

Durrant, W. and Durrant, A., 1968. *The Lessons of History.* https://www. simonandschuster.com.au/books/The-Lessons-of-History/Will-Durant/ 9781439170199.

IIyushina, N., 2023. Work for Decentralized Autonomous Organization: What Empirical Labour Economics Can Tell Us about the Decentralized Digital Workforce. *Journal of the British Blockchain Association.* https://jbba.sch olasticahq.com/article/81103.

Lommers, K., Ghanchi, M., Ngo, K., Song, Q., and Xu, J., DAO Accounting. 2023. *Working Paper.* https://papers.ssrn.com/sol3/papers.cfm?abstract_ id=4200414.

Lumineau, F., Wang, W., and Schilke, O., 2021. Blockchain Governance — A New Way of Organizing Collaborations? *Organization Science.* https://pubsonl ine.informs.org/doi/10.1287/orsc.2020.1379.

Makaridis, C., Froewis, M., Sridhar, K., and Böhme, R., 2021. The Rise of Decentralized Cryptocurrency Exchanges: Evaluating the Role of Airdrops and Governance Tokens. *Working Paper.* https://papers.ssrn.com/sol3/ papers.cfm?abstract_id=3915140.

North, D., 1991. Institutions. *Journal of Economic Perspectives.* https://www. aeaweb.org/articles?id=10.1257/jep.5.1.97.

Ohlhaver, P., Weyl, G., and Buterin, V., 2022. Decentralized Society: Finding Web3's Soul. *Working Paper.* https://papers.ssrn.com/sol3/papers.cfm? abstract_id=4105763.

Peña-Calvin, A., Saldivar, J., Arroyo, J., and Hassan, S., 2023. A Categorization of Decentralized Autonomous Organizations: The Case of the Aragon Platform. *IEEE Transactions on Computational Social Systems.* https:// ieeexplore.ieee.org/document/10217072?signout=success.

Schoonwinkel, H., 2023. Towards Fair Presentation of DAO Treasuries: An Evaluation of Native Governance Token Reporting Practices. *The Journal of British Blockchain Association.* https://jbba.scholasticahq.com/article/ 77534-towards-fair-presentation-of-dao-treasuries-an-evaluation-of-native- governance-token-reporting-practices.

Williamsom, O., 1985. *The Economic Institutions of Capitalism.* https://www. simonandschuster.com/books/The-Economic-Intstitutions-of-Capitalism/ Oliver-E-Williamson/9780684863740.

Ziegler, C. and Welpe, I., 2022. A Taxonomy of Decentralized Autonomous Organizations. *ICIS 2022 Proceedings.* https://aisel.aisnet.org/icis2022/ blockchain/blockchain/1.

Chapter 5

A DAO Risk Assessment Methodology for Financial Services Professionals

Abstract

This chapter introduces our risk assessment methodology with six risk categories inherent to the structure and operation of decentralized autonomous organizations (DAOs): accountability, community, financial, governance, operational, and technology risks. It provides detailed explanations and real-world examples to illustrate the potential impact of these risks on financial institutions engaging with DAOs. It also introduces a simple mathematical model for aggregating individual risk scores into an overall DAO risk score, which can inform the decision-making process for interacting with DAOs as a client or service provider. Finally, the chapter emphasizes the importance of continuous monitoring, regular model validation, and risk reporting to ensure effective risk management when engaging with DAOs.

5.1 Introduction

This chapter surfaces the risks inherent in DAOs, specifically from the perspective of financial services professionals who are looking to interact with them. Financial institutions engage with different parties. They purchase services from vendors, and they service clients. Client and vendor onboarding are critical processes to establish trust, ensure compliance, and mitigate risks.[1] In the traditional financial system, certain elements of client onboarding are non-negotiable. These include thorough Know Your Client (KYC) procedures, anti-money laundering (AML) checks, and counter-terrorism financing (CTF). Financial institutions are required to collect and verify counterparty information, such as identity, address, source of funds, and beneficial ownership. Failure to adhere to these stringent requirements can result in severe regulatory and reputational consequences. DAOs present unique challenges for financial institutions in terms of onboarding as their members are often pseudonymous or anonymous. Moreover, the governance structure of DAOs, which relies on smart contracts and token-based voting, differs significantly from the hierarchical decision-making processes in traditional organizations. But these are not the only challenges to consider.

In our DAO risk assessment methodology (Fig. 5.1), we recommend a four-step approach.

First, we identify and define the idiosyncratic risks inherent in DAOs, which are accountability risk, community risk, financial risk, governance risk, operational risk, and technology risk. Second, we assess the risks using a probability and impact matrix. Third, we show how to decide whether to onboard. If the decision is to proceed, then the fourth step is to monitor and control the relationship. By understanding and mitigating these risks, financial institutions can unlock the potential benefits of partnering with these innovative structures while maintaining the highest standards of security and compliance.

Financial services firms have their own methodologies for assessing counterparty and credit risk for existing types of clients. For example, a bank will assess the business model of a client. Given the nascent and developing nature of DAOs, what we offer in this section is a methodology to assess the idiosyncratic risks that arise

---

[1] https://www.reedsmith.com/en/perspectives/2023/06/managing-dao-related-risks#:~:text=DAO%20voting%20rights%20allocated%20by,to%20their%20history%20or%20status (accessed on 5 June 2024).

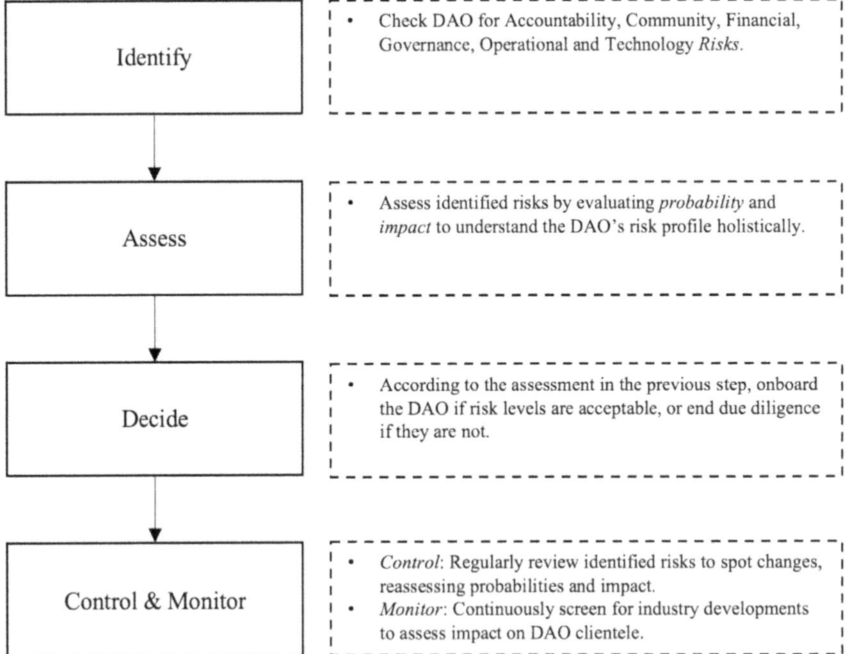

Fig. 5.1. DAO risk assessment methodology.

from the nature of DAOs. It is important to note that developments in the DAO and blockchain space are happening rapidly, at both the technological and regulatory levels. As such, the risks listed in this chapter will not be exhaustive nor conclusive. Lastly, legal risk is an important area for DAOs. As both authors are not lawyers, we cover legal risk-related questions in Chapter 7 via an interview with a lawyer.

5.2 Identify

Although some of the risks described in this section will sound familiar to the financial services professional, our contribution is to highlight how these risks are different and idiosyncratic in the DAO context (Table 5.1).

Table 5.1. DAO risk types.

Risk	Definition
DAO accountability risk	It is the risk of not being able to clearly identify a representative responsible for the DAO and its members' actions.
DAO community risk	It is the risk of failing to attract, engage, and retain community members.
DAO financial risk	It is the risk that the DAO fails to meet its financial obligations due to the inappropriate level of diversification in its treasury portfolio.
DAO governance risk	It is the risk of the DAO's decision-making process becoming dysfunctional.
DAO operational risk	It is the risk of loss resulting from inadequate or failed processes, people, and systems or from external events.
DAO technology risk	It is a type of operational risk resulting from blockchain and related infrastructure outages or malfunctions.

5.2.1 *A definition of DAO accountability risk*

DAO accountability risk is the risk of not being able to clearly identify a representative responsible for the DAO and its members' actions.

In traditional firms, CEOs and directors represent the company. When something goes wrong, it is possible to identify accountable individuals. The details of the responsible CEO or director of the company are always known. In contrast, most DAOs have no CEO or directors to represent them. At a minimum, DAO members can be identified by their wallet addresses. However, a wallet address does not reveal any information about the person's identity in the physical world. Some wallet addresses are tied to social media profiles, for example, on LinkedIn, X (formerly known as Twitter), or Instagram. But it is important to remember that many social media profiles are pseudonymous. There are some DAOs that might require their members to reveal their social media accounts as verification to join. The most complete form of identification is to ask for physical world identification, for example, passports. At the time of writing,

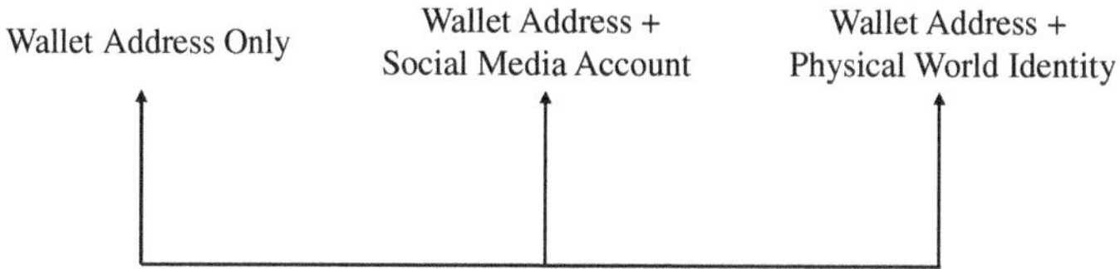

Fig. 5.2. Identifiability spectrum.

it is not common for DAOs to ask for such ID. Figure 5.2 shows the spectrum of identifiability of persons in DAO membership.

5.2.2 *A definition of DAO community risk*

> DAO community risk is the risk of failing to attract, engage, and retain community members.

The viability and success of a DAO depend on its members. Hence, when assessing community risk, we look at the participation and engagement levels of the members, as these are the factors that will affect whether a DAO is able to achieve its goals. Laturnus (2023) finds that DAOs with greater participation rates in voting are associated with superior performance where performance is measured in market capitalization in USD. When making a judgment on the sustainability of a DAO as part of the onboarding process, it is important to understand how the DAO is attracting, engaging, and incentivizing its community.

Originally, creating DAOs using smart contracts on the blockchain required programming skills. The emergence of platforms such as Aragon, DAOHaus, and Colony has made it easier for non-coders to launch DAOs in recent years. However, joining a DAO is still not a mainstream activity, and some wallet management skills are required. Many DAO platforms can be challenging to navigate because of their technical nature. Hence, attracting new members can be a challenge. After they join, DAO members must keep up with many aspects of the operations, including, for example, the governance mechanism, tokenomics, and the DAO's objectives. Novel governance features and voting mechanisms, e.g. quadratic voting, are appealing for their experimental nature in governance, but at the same time, they can also be overwhelmingly complex to members. Such technical hurdles adversely affect broad adoption, and a challenging user experience can further dampen participation and engagement.

The current web tools used for assessing DAO community engagement are still limited in functionality. DeepDAO gives us activity metrics that include the number of token holders, the number of tokens a member holds, the number of monthly proposals and votes, and the details of each proposal (who proposed and how many voters voted for and against, and abstained).[2] There are other metrics that help to indicate the quality of community engagement, such as the frequency and quality of discussions in the DAO's forums and attendance at community calls and meetings. However, these metrics might be less easily obtained. As noted in Chapter 4, current statistics show high levels of voter apathy. DAOs must constantly find new ways to improve voter participation to increase their longevity.

5.2.3   *A definition of DAO financial risk*

> DAO financial risk is the risk that the DAO fails to meet its financial obligations due to the inappropriate level of diversification in its treasury portfolio.

In traditional corporate finance, treasury management plays a pivotal role in ensuring the sustainability of a firm's business model by being able to pay for liabilities and investing excess capital at an attractive rate in line with the entity's risk appetite. Decades of research, multiple strategies, countless tools, and technology as well as rigorous regulations have shaped the development of treasury management in corporations. In comparison, DAO Treasury Management is still in its infancy. A DAO's treasury is comparable to a traditional company's balance sheet in the sense that it plays a crucial role in its ability to meet financial obligations.

---

[2]https://deepdao.io/organizations (accessed on 16 February 2024).

A well-managed treasury typically maintains a strong financial position, ensures sufficient liquidity, and manages risks effectively to meet financial obligations without major disruption. Part of the process also involves diversifying the treasury portfolio. Some of these aspects of a well-run, mature treasury operation are not present in the nascent world of DAOs.

At the inception of a DAO, the main way for it to raise funds is to create its own token. Therefore, for many DAOs, the token is the main source of funding. It probably does not come as a surprise that a study (Schellinger *et al.*, 2023) of the 20 largest DAO treasuries reveals that over 81% of total treasuries' assets are held in the native DAO token. According to the study, other crypto tokens held by the DAO treasuries are stablecoins (7.7%), ETH (8.7%), and other tokens (1.8%). This high concentration exposes DAO treasuries to crypto price fluctuations and volatility. DAOs have ongoing costs that include development, engineering, operations, legal compliance, and infrastructure. If their treasuries are not prudently managed, the financial risk of the DAO defaulting on their obligations increases.

Despite the headline figures that show that DAO treasuries are concentrated in holding their own tokens, different DAOs have their proprietary asset allocation strategies. Some DAOs chose to hold a higher percentage in stablecoins versus the more volatile ETH, and hence a DAO treasury that has a larger exposure to ETH would be more susceptible to crypto-market volatility than one that holds a higher amount of a stablecoin. Increasingly, some DAOs are looking to diversify away from crypto-assets and into real-world assets (RWAs), for example, money market funds, real estate, traditional securities, and hedge funds. Given the wide range of RWAs, the choice of which RWA a DAO chooses will influence its impact on the treasury. MakerDAO and Aave have diversified into buying and holding US Treasuries.[3,4] In terms of credit risk,

---

[3] https://www.coindesk.com/markets/2023/06/01/makerdao-paves-way-for-addi tional-128b-us-treasury-purchase (accessed on 16 April 2024).
[4] https://governance.aave.com/t/arfc-aave-treasury-rwa-allocation/14790 (acc essed on 17 April 2024).

the US government is one of the most highly rated. In terms of interest rate risk, the volatility of treasuries is comparably lower than that of crypto and offers diversification.

What we highlight as financial risks are also potential opportunities for financial services professionals. For example, DAO treasuries will benefit immensely from portfolio and balance sheet management expertise. To lower the volatility of the portfolio, stablecoins currently are the asset of choice for crypto-native entities. However, traditional financial services professionals who can interact with DAOs can introduce other low-volatility RWAs for DAOs to consider as part of portfolio diversification.

5.2.4 *A definition of DAO governance risk*

> DAO governance risk is the risk of the DAO's decision-making processes becoming dysfunctional.

There can be several reasons for a dysfunctional governance process. One reason could be as simple as the DAO members not being familiar with the process. For example, at the launch of the new Uniswap governance module, some proposers did not follow the three-step process for approving a proposal. Their proposal failed, and DAO members were not able to make a decision.

But there are other more hostile reasons: One incident to illustrate such type of risk is the example of Beanstalk. Beanstalk is a DeFi protocol that issued the USD algorithmic stablecoin with the ticker BEAN$. An attacker took out a loan to buy Beanstalk's governance token (STALK$) that gave them 67% of all voting rights. With their supermajority stake, the attacker voted to execute a proposal that transferred assets from the Beanstalk treasury to the attacker's wallet. After selling these assets and repaying the loan, the attacker netted USD 80 million in profit, and the stablecoin BEAN$ fell 75% in value, effectively destroying its value proposition.

Attackers could also spam the governance system with proposals, making it difficult for the community to distinguish which proposals are worth reviewing in detail and which ones are better categorized as spam. This is known as a Sybil attack. The attacker creates a large number of wallet addresses to gain disproportionate influence in a DAO.

Philip Daian and coauthors first introduced the concept of a DarkDAO in a blog post, defining it as a decentralized cartel that buys on-chain votes opaquely.[5] DarkDAOs engage in a vote-buying attack to subvert another DAO. In its simplest form, a DarkDAO is a smart contract that pays its members to use their voting power in other DAOs. DarkDAOs operate in an opaque fashion; their members are indistinguishable from regular DAO members. DarkDAO membership cannot be proven. Lastly, DarkDAOs operate under a bounded scope; the members do not contribute any additional resources except for their vote and pre-agreed-upon costs, for example, related transaction costs (Austgen *et al.*, 2023). This attack is somewhat similar to "empty voting" that hedge funds conduct to influence voting outcomes without owning an economic interest in the company as they borrow shares to vote and repay.

Apart from attackers, there are other sources of DAO governance risk. Suppose a vote triggers a dispute resolution process, and the parties involved cannot resolve their disagreement. The lack of resolution may adversely affect the continuous governance process. The examples in this section do not cover all sources of DAO governance risk but pinpoint the type of issues that a financial services firm might want to critically assess before deciding to collaborate with a DAO.

5.2.5 *A definition of DAO operational risk*

> DAO operational risk is the risk of loss resulting from inadequate or failed processes, people, systems or from external events.

The Bank of International Settlements (BIS) defined operational risk in their 2011 article "as the risk of loss resulting from inadequate

---

[5]https://hackingdistributed.com/2018/07/02/on-chain-vote-buying (accessed on 15 May 2024).

or failed internal processes, people, systems or from external events (...)."[6] The definition is comprehensive enough to be used in the context of DAOs. However, we will use examples to highlight DAO-specific operational risks.

For a DAO, operational risks range from the failure of internal processes to problems that arise from the intersection of on-chain and off-chain worlds. A DAO's purpose might be to fund academic research focused on a particular topic, perhaps climate change, longevity, or AI. The actual work happens off-chain, but its status needs to synchronize with the blockchain eventually which is where data inconsistency can cause issues.

Human errors are another form of operational risk. One example is when a DAO treasury manager falls for a Vanity Address Attack (VAA).[7] The VAA is a technique malicious actors use to deceive blockchain users to send funds to the wrong address. While blockchain addresses are typically generated randomly, tools like Vanity-ETH allow users to create personalized addresses with specific character sequences. Attackers use these tools to create an address that closely resembles a target user's address. This is how the attack works: The attacker identifies a target user by monitoring the blockchain's mempool, which holds pending transactions. Using automated bots and sufficient computing power, the attacker quickly generates a vanity address that matches the first and last few characters of the target's address. The attacker then sends a small amount of cryptocurrency (dust) to the target's wallet, causing the transaction to appear at the top of their transaction history on etherscan.io. Suppose the target user is not vigilant and only checks the address's first and last few characters when making their next transaction. In this case, they may inadvertently copy the attacker's vanity address instead of their own. As a result, the user ends up sending a large amount of funds to the attacker's wallet. To prevent

---

[6]https://www.bis.org/publ/bcbs195.pdf (accessed on 9 April 2024).

[7]https://www.isaca.org/resources/news-and-trends/isaca-now-blog/2024/vanity-gone-rogue-the-rise-of-exploits-targeting-custom-blockchain-addresses (accessed on 6 June 2024).

falling victim to VAA, users must carefully check the entire address when conducting transactions and not rely solely on the initial and final characters displayed by wallet software like Metamask.

In the DAO context, external events can relate to the demise of a critical service provider for the DAO. Imagine a DAO uses a payments company that also provides a stablecoin product to its customers. The DAO treasury holds a significant percentage of its reserves in this stablecoin, and the payments company fails. As a result, the stablecoin loses its USD peg and its value swiftly trends toward zero, wiping out much of the DAO's reserves.

Operational risks are not limited to the examples above, but these provide a flavor of the types of operational risks possible in the DAO context.

5.2.6 *A definition of DAO technology risk*

> DAO technology risk is a type of operational risk resulting from blockchain and related infrastructure outages or malfunctions.

Typically, when a founder sets up a new company in the off-chain world, there is a regulatory authority to turn to. For example, in Singapore, the Accounting and Corporate Regulatory Authority (ACRA) is the regulator for business registration. In contrast, DAOs are organizations built on top of blockchain platforms in the form of smart contracts. As such, one source of risk originates from underlying technologies on which DAOs depend. We have described several characteristics of blockchains that are important to understand and are sources of DAO technology risk in Chapter 2. Note that our definition covers both outages and malfunctions of technology. We define an outage as the unavailability of the system or the severe degradation of its service that it usually provides to users. An example of an outage is when a blockchain stops validating transactions and adding new blocks to the chain. A slightly less severe but still very harmful situation is a degradation of service. For example, imagine an attacker spamming a blockchain with transactions and congesting the network. This service degradation will slow down the service a DAO provides to its members.

Malfunctions of technology occur when the system performs in an unintended or unexpected way. To illustrate malfunctions, imagine a blockchain oracle that usually provides reliable price information to a blockchain. Before we move on, let's delve a bit deeper into the topic of oracles. Smart contracts can only access data stored within the blockchain network they exist on. Many applications, particularly in finance, require oracles to control the execution of business logic. Imagine a smart futures contract on gold: To price the future, we need the price of the underlying asset, gold. An oracle is an interface that delivers data from external data outside a blockchain to a smart contract to consume (Beniiche, 2020). Through an oracle, the required data can be retrieved from a trustworthy API provided by companies like Bloomberg or Reuters and fed into the smart futures contract. While oracles are a relatively new concept, empirical research shows that the existence of oracles in an ecosystem is positively associated with the platform's total value locked (TVL) and the valuation of its token due to positive network effects (Cong *et al.*, 2024). Oracles are critical to interoperability between different platforms and the off-chain world. A prominent decentralized oracle platform is Chainlink.[8] Now, back to the example of a malfunction: one day, an oracle suffers from a bug in its code and feeds the wrong price to a blockchain. If a DAO depends on these prices to function or make decisions, it can have a cascading impact on the DAO's operations.

5.3 Assessing DAO risk

5.3.1 *Introduction*

Our objective in this section is to present a high-level methodology for assessing DAO risk from the perspective of financial services institutions. At this stage, there are two ways for both parties to engage. First, a financial services provider can offer their services to a DAO. For example, a bank could offer payments- and working

---

[8]https://chain.link (accessed on 13 May 2024).

capital-related services to a DAO. Second, a financial services provider can use a DAO's platform, effectively becoming the DAO's customer. For example, a brokerage firm could use a decentralized exchange to offer cryptocurrency execution services to its clients. Our risk assessment methodology will cover both engagement models.

To show the potential impact of interacting with a DAO, it is critical to reflect on the relevant functions of a financial institution. We divide these functions into infrastructure, risk, and strategy (Table 5.2).

Within infrastructure, financial institutions uphold operational efficiency through processes spanning transaction processing, account management, and customer relations. Concurrently, robust technology infrastructure underpins these operations, encompassing networks of IT systems and applications that facilitate banking functions. In dealing with DAOs, this includes wallet management to handle digital assets.

Within the risk function, institutions implement methodologies to manage distinct types of risk. The credit area oversight extends from lending practices to portfolio management, protecting the firm from risks beyond its appetite or those it cannot accept from a regulatory perspective. The computer security area safeguards the integrity of the institution's information systems and data, protecting against cyber threats and unauthorized access. Financial crime-related activities and processes combat money laundering and fraud and ensure compliance with global sanctions. For market exposure, the institution manages its risk exposure to market fluctuations, for example, risks stemming from interest rates and foreign exchange dynamics or commodities markets. Regulatory compliance ensures adherence to the ever-evolving regulatory frameworks of central banks and financial services regulators across jurisdictions. The management of an institution's reputation is also critical. Stakeholder confidence hinges upon effectively managing its public image and brand, resonating with stakeholders and the broader public. While some of the existing risk management tools can be used in the context of DAOs, expanding the scope of the business area by analyzing the DAO risks introduced in the previous section is indispensable.

Table 5.2. Financial institution functions and areas.

Function	Area
Infrastructure	Operations
	Technology
Risk	Credit
	Computer security
	Financial crime
	Market exposure
	Regulatory compliance
	Reputation
Strategy	Planning

Within strategy, management plans for and tracks against future growth and resilience deliverables, articulating the institution's strategic vision and identifying avenues for sustainable development and long-term success. In a future where more communities will use DAOs to collaborate, having a strategy to engage these new entities seems prudent.

Rather than reinventing risk management and control instruments, we adhere to well-known tools and best practices. For example, the risk matrix (Garvey and Lansdowne, 1998) is a valuable tool for assessing qualitative risks that require a fair amount of judgment and is suitable for our context of emerging DAO risk management. A risk matrix plots a risk's impact on the x-axis and the risk's probability on the y-axis. A risk manager can define a consistent scale for both axes. In our example in Figure 5.3, we use a three-point scale for simplicity's sake, but one may choose to extend to four-point or five-point scales for additional granularity. Our scale choice creates a 3×3 matrix (low (1)/medium (2)/high (3)) with nine spaces and three risk levels. The essential idea behind the risk matrix is that it allows us to think separately about a qualitative risk in terms of impact and probability. Only after doing so can we calculate a risk score by multiplying the impact and probability scores.

DAO Risk matrix

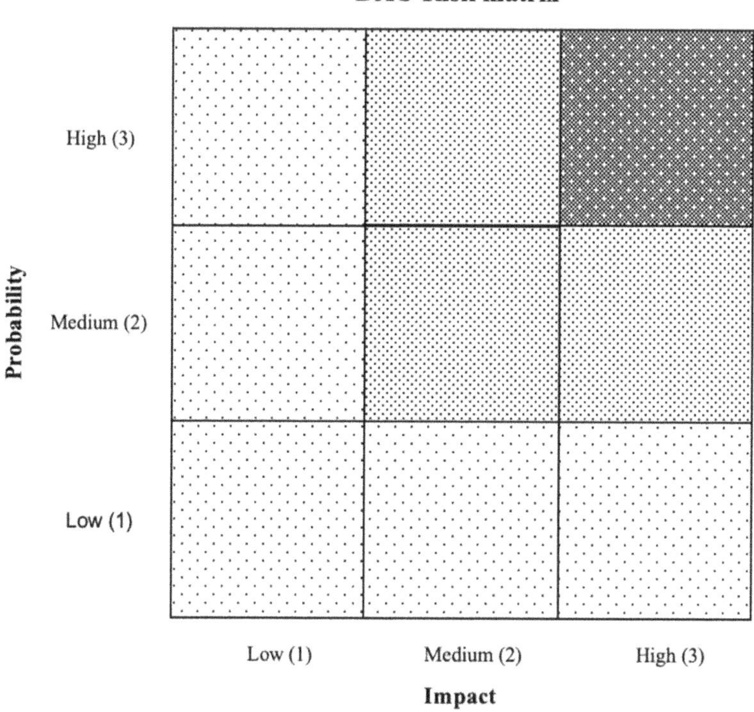

Fig. 5.3. DAO risk matrix.

In the following sections, we complement the risk matrix with legend tables that illustrate high, medium, and low levels of impact and probability for the six DAO risks on the financial institution's functions and areas. These examples will help familiarize with the risk management task at hand and can be a starting point to develop a more comprehensive and custom matrix.

5.3.2 *Assessing DAO accountability risk*

In Table 5.3, we describe the impact and probability levels for a DAO's accountability risk. We use a mix of real and fictitious examples to illustrate the different levels of this risk in a more tangible way.

Table 5.3. DAO accountability risk matrix legend.

Risk type: Accountability risk is the risk of not being able to clearly identify a representative responsible for the DAO and its members' actions.			
		Impact definition	**Probability definition**
	High	Severe impact on the financial institution's reputation, regulatory compliance and financial crime areas resulting from accountability-related issues with the DAO and its members. Example: A fund manager invests in a DAO. Subsequently a significant holder of the DAO token who is also an active participant of the DAO governance process is exposed as a terrorist. Impact: 3	Frequent occurrence of accountability-related issues within the DAO due to not being able to clearly identify a representative responsible for the DAO and its members' actions. Probability: 3
	Medium	Moderate impact on the financial institution's reputation and regulatory compliance areas resulting from accountability-related issues with the DAO and its members. Example: A payments service provider assists a DAO to purchase physical art. Subsequently, one of the prominent DAO members is exposed as laundering money through the acquisition of the art. Impact: 2	Occasional occurrence of accountability-related issues within the DAO due to not being able to clearly identify a representative responsible for the DAO and its members' actions. Probability: 2
	Low	No to minimal impact on the financial institution's reputation and regulatory compliance areas resulting from accountability-related issues with the DAO and its members. Example: An ESG conscious investment firm manages part of a DAO's treasury portfolio. Subsequently, the DAO switches to an energy-intensive smart contract platform, which goes against the investment firm's values. Impact: 1	No to rare occurrence of accountability-related issues within the DAO due to not being able to clearly identify a representative responsible for the DAO and its members' actions. Probability: 1

5.3.3 *Assessing DAO community risk*

In Table 5.4, we describe the impact and probability levels for a DAO's community risk. We use a mix of real and fictitious examples to illustrate the different levels of this risk in a more tangible way.

5.3.4 *Assessing DAO financial risk*

In Table 5.5, we describe the impact and probability levels for a DAO's financial risk. We use a mix of real and fictitious examples to illustrate the different levels of this risk in a more tangible way.

5.3.5 *Assessing DAO governance risk*

In Table 5.6, we describe the impact and probability levels for a DAO's governance risk. We use a mix of real and fictitious examples to illustrate the different levels of this risk in a more tangible way.

Table 5.4. DAO community risk matrix legend.

Risk type: Community risk is the risk of the DAO failing to attract, engage, and retain community members.			
		Impact definition	**Probability definition**
	High	Severe impact on the financial institution's operations, reputation and strategy areas resulting from community-related issues with the DAO and its members. Example: The financial institution offers the DAO's products or services to their clients in a material way. When a DAO loses its community members, it will fail to deliver its services. Impact: 3	Frequent occurrence of community-related issues within the DAO due its failure to attract, engage and retain community members. Probability: 3
	Medium	Moderate impact on the financial institution's operations and strategy areas resulting from community-related issues with the DAO and its members. Example: The financial institution uses the DAO's products or services internally. When the DAO has diminishing membership, its delivery of services will be delayed and less reliable. Impact: 2	Occasional occurrence of community-related issues within the DAO due its failure to attract, engage and retain community members. Probability: 2
	Low	No to minimal impact on the financial institution's operations and strategy areas resulting from community-related issues with the DAO and its members. Example: The financial institution does not have significant ties or exposure to the DAO. The DAO loses its members slowly over time but can maintain a minimal level of service. Impact: 1	No to rare occurrence of community-related issues within the DAO due its failure to attract, engage and retain community members. Probability: 1

5.3.6 *Assessing DAO operational risk*

In Table 5.7, we describe the impact and probability levels for a DAO's operational risk. We use a mix of real and fictitious examples to illustrate the different levels of this risk in a more tangible way.

5.3.7 *Assessing DAO technology risk*

In Table 5.8, we describe the impact and probability levels for a DAO's technology risk. We use a mix of real and fictitious examples to illustrate the different levels of this risk in a more tangible way.

Table 5.5. DAO financial risk matrix legend.

		Impact	Probability
	High	Severe impact on the financial institution's credit and market exposure areas resulting from finance-related issues of the DAO. Example: The bank made a significant loan to the DAO. Because of its weak treasury portfolio management, the DAO fails to meet all its financial obligations, including the loan to the bank. Impact: 3	Frequent occurrence of finance-related issues within the DAO due to difficulties in meeting its financial obligations. Probability: 3
	Medium	Moderate impact on the financial institution's credit and market exposure resulting from finance-related issues of the DAO. Example: The bank has a mid-tier cash management client that is a DAO. Because of the DAOs weak treasury portfolio management, it fails and is no longer the bank's client. Impact: 2	Occasional occurrence of finance-related issues within the DAO in meeting financial obligations. Probability: 2
	Low	No to minimal impact on the financial institution's valuation and exposure to the DAO resulting from finance-related issues of the DAO. Example: The DAO is an insignificant FX client of a broker. Because of the DAOs weak treasury portfolio management, it fails, and the broker loses the fee income. Impact: 1	No to rare occurrence of finance-related issues within the DAO in meeting financial obligations. Probability: 1

Risk type: Financial risk is the risk that the it fails to meet its financial obligations due to the inappropriate level of diversification in its treasury portfolio.

5.4 Decide

In this next part of the DAO risk management methodology, we introduce a method to help financial services organizations aggregate a DAO's idiosyncratic risks and calculate an overall DAO risk score. This simple approach allows institutions to assign different weights to DAO risks according to their preferences. The aggregation process is illustrated as follows:

$$\Pi\ \text{DAOrisk} \approx \Sigma a\text{Ar} + b\text{Cr} + c\text{Fr} + d\text{Gr} + e\text{Or} + f\text{Tr},$$

where Ar denotes the accountability DAO risk score, Cr the community DAO risk score, Fr the financial DAO risk score, Gr the

Table 5.6. DAO governance risk matrix legend.

Risk type: Governance risk is the risk of a DAO's decision-making processes becoming dysfunctional.			
		Impact definition	**Probability definition**
	High	Severe impact on the financial institution's strategic and reputational areas resulting from governance-related issues with the DAO and its members. Example: A large private bank has incorporated a DeFi exchange into its client platform. A DarkDAO then attacks the DeFi exchange DAO by successfully voting on a proposal to stop the collaboration, forcing the private bank to stop offering the service to clients. Impact: 3	Frequent occurrence of governance-related issues within the DAO due to decision-making processes becoming dysfunctional. Probability: 3
	Medium	Moderate impact on the financial institution's strategic area resulting from governance-related issues with the DAO and its members. Example: A brokerage firm uses a DeFi derivatives protocol. The broker raises a governance proposal for a new functionality to be implemented on the platform. The proposal would benefit the broker and its users. However, due to high voting power concentrated in two token holders who would not benefit, the proposal gets rejected. Impact: 2	Occasional occurrence of governance issues within the DAO due to decision-making processes becoming dysfunctional. Probability: 2
	Low	No to minimal impact on on the financial institution's strategic area resulting from governance-related issues with the DAO and its members. Example: A fund manager regularly borrows on a DAO-governed decentralized lending platform. The fund manager requests a new functionality by raising a proposal. Due to low voter participation, the new functionality does not get approved, but the platform remains operational. Impact: 1	No to rare occurrence of governance issues within the DAO due to decision-making processes becoming dysfunctional. Probability: 1

Table 5.7. DAO operational risk matrix legend.

Risk type: Operational risk is the risk of loss resulting from inadequate or failed processes, people, and systems or from external events.			
		Impact definition	**Probability definition**
	High	Severe impact on the financial institution's credit, operational and financial crime areas resulting from operational issues with the DAO and its members. Example: An exchange uses a DAO's DeFi services. A rogue DAO member launders illicit funds on behalf of sanctioned entities by selling part of the treasury's cryptocurrency into fiat money on the exchange. Impact: 3	Frequent occurrence of operational issues within the DAO due to inadequate or failed processes, people, and systems or from external events. Probability: 3
	Medium	Moderate impact on the financial institution's credit, operational and financial crime areas resulting from operational issues with the DAO and its members. Example: A DAO is a lender's client. A DAO member in charge of treasury management falls for the vanity address attack (VAA). The attack triggers a large loss, effectively disabling the DAO from making payments to the lender. Impact: 2	Occasional occurrence of operational issues within the DAO due to inadequate or failed processes, people, and systems or from external events. Probability: 2
	Low	No to minimal impact on the financial institution's credit, operational and financial crime areas resulting from operational issues with the DAO and its members. Example: A DAO engages in work offchain. The DAO's members clean up plastics from beaches and get rewarded for their effort. The amounts due get misreported onchain and hence earnings to the DAO are lower than expected, making the DAO less profitable than planned. Impact: 1	No to rare occurrence of operational issues within the DAO due to inadequate or failed processes, people, and systems or from external events. Probability: 1

Table 5.8. DAO technology risk matrix legend.

		Impact definition	Probability definition
Risk type: Technology risk of a DAO is a type of operational risk resulting from blockchain and related infrastructure outages or malfunctions.			
	High	Severe impact on the financial institution's operational, IT security and reputational areas resulting from technology-related issues with the DAO and its members. Example: A brokerage uses a DAO's services to offer execution services to its clients. The DAO built their DApp on a smart contract platform that continuously has total system outages, making the services unavailable. Impact: 3	Frequent occurrence of technology-related issues within the DAO due to blockchain and related infrastructure outages or malfunctions. Probability: 3
	Medium	Moderate impact on the financial institution's operational, IT security and reputational areas resulting from technology-related issues with the DAO and its members. Example: An insurance company uses a DAO's DApp that is built on a smart contract with highly variable gas fees. The cost of using the service cannot be estimated which makes building a sustainable business model very difficult. Impact: 2	Occasional occurrence of technology issues with the DAO due to blockchain and related infrastructure outages or malfunctions. Probability: 2
	Low	No to minimal impact on the financial institution's operational, IT security and reputational areas resulting from technology-related issues with the DAO and its members. Example: A bank uses a DAO's platform that offers cross-border payment services. The underlying smart contract is highly susceptible to maximum extractable value (MEV) activity that imposes a small tax on every transaction, lowering the margin of the bank. Impact: 1	No to rare occurrence of technology issues with the DAO due to blockchain and related infrastructure outages or malfunctions. Probability: 1

governance DAO risk score, Or the operational DAO risk score, Tr the technology DAO risk score, and $\Sigma a, b, c, d, e, f \equiv 1$ expresses the weights financial institutions can assign according to their DAO risk appetite (Fig. 5.4).

Now that we have introduced a simple tool as a starting point on how to aggregate DAO risks and create a score for a particular prospective DAO client or service provider, the appropriate body needs to decide whether to onboard or not. Risk managers could further develop frameworks that involve certain thresholds for acceptance or rejection to facilitate this decision. For example, depending on the financial institution's risk appetite, it could set an overall score as a prerequisite for onboarding. Risk managers may also include K.O. criteria that will stop the firm from onboarding a DAO if a single risk makes the DAO counterparty unacceptable despite all other risk scores being rated low. Managing DAO-related risks does not end with onboarding. Financial institutions need to monitor

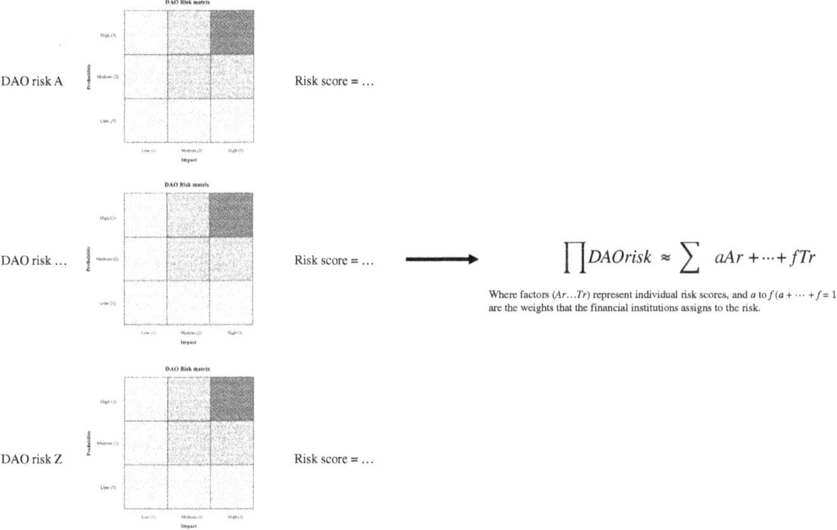

Fig. 5.4. DAO risk aggregation.

and control continuously, which is what the following section briefly covers.

5.5 Monitor and control

In addition to identifying and assessing DAO-related risks, additional steps are critical to managing its risks over time for a financial institution. The steps are regular model validation, continuous monitoring, and reporting. These steps enable the financial institution to remain adaptable, track risk levels against established limits, detect potential risk events, and keep stakeholders informed about the firm's risk profile. Regular validation and back-testing are essential to ensure the accuracy and reliability of risk measurement models. Validation involves comparing the model's predictions with actual outcomes and making necessary adjustments to enhance the model's performance. Continuous risk monitoring is of particular importance when engaging with DAOs, as they are fast-evolving and pivot much faster than large corporations. The financial institution must monitor risk levels against established risk appetite and limits based on previous sections on identification and risk assessment. Adding DAO-related key risk indicators (KRIs) to the firm's existing risk monitoring system is the most efficient and effective way to holistically track and detect potential risk events. Regular risk reporting to senior management and the board is crucial for informed decision-making and oversight. Risk reports should cover various aspects, including risk metrics, limits, risk trends, stress test results, and compliance with regulatory requirements as they develop. Reporting should also include qualitative assessments of emerging risks and the effectiveness of risk mitigation measures.

Any discussion on risk should end with a cautionary final note. In the book *The Illusion of Control: Why Financial Crises Happen, and What We Can (and Can't) Do About It*, Danielsson (2022) argues that financial markets are inherently unpredictable and that attempts to control or predict them often lead to a false sense of security. Often, "the models we use to manage risk often give us a false sense of security. They work well when markets are calm but fail spectacularly when we need them most." In our context of DAOs, this implies going beyond collecting data and calculating scores. For example, regular interaction with members, on social media platforms and in person, may be a good way to complement the DAO risk methodology we propose.

References

Austgen, J., Fabrega, A., Allen, S., Babel, K., Kelkar, M., and Juels, A., 2023. DAO Decentralization: Voting-Bloc Entropy, Bribery, and Dark DAOs. *arXiv Electronic Journal*. https://arxiv.org/abs/2311.03530.

Beniiche, A., 2020. A Study of Blockchain Oracles. *Working Paper*. https://arxiv.org/abs/2004.07140.

Cong, W., Prasad, E., and Rabetti, D., 2024. Financial and Informational Integration Through Oracle Networks. *Working Paper*. https://papers.ssrn.com/sol3/papers.cfm?abstract_id=4495514.

Danielsson, J., 2022. *The Illusion of Control: Why Financial Crises Happen, and What We Can (and Can't) Do About It*. https://yalebooks.yale.edu/book/9780300234817/the-illusion-of-control.

Garvey, P.R. and Lansdowne, Z.F., 1998. *Risk Matrix: An Approach for Identifying, Assessing, and Ranking Program Risks.* https://books.google.com.au/books?hl=en&lr=&id=K7XvC2q4oVIC&oi=fnd&pg=PA18&ots=51Eht7DuP&sig=Nqi0N7t5tM_JYyrjyadyDjtTxdw&redir_esc=y#v=onepage&q&f=false.

Laturnus, V., 2023. The Economics of Decentralized Autonomous Organizations. *Working Paper.* https://papers.ssrn.com/sol3/papers.cfm?abstract_id=4320196.

Schellinger, B., Fiedler, I., and Steinmetz, F., 2023. How Are You DAOing? The State of DAO Treasuries. *Working Paper.* https://papers.ssrn.com/sol3/papers.cfm?abstract_id=4604968.

Chapter 6

Two DAO Case Studies

Abstract
This chapter analyzes two case studies, MakerDAO and KlimaDAO, to
explore the risks inherent in DAOs and provide insights for financial
services firms considering collaboration. For each case study, the chapter
investigates six risk categories: accountability, community, financial,
governance, operational, and technology risks. In the MakerDAO case
study, the DAO is assumed to be a brokerage client. The KlimaDAO
case study assumes that the DAO is a cash management client.

Based on the examples of MakerDAO and KlimaDAO, we reveal the
challenges and opportunities for financial services firms considering
interacting with DAOs. First, we give some context of the value
proposition of the organization. Then, for each case study, we system-
atically investigate six critical DAO risk categories: accountability
risk, community risk, financial risk, governance risk, operational risk,
and technology risk, as defined in the previous chapter. The aim is
to uncover valuable insights to inform a financial institution's risk
function. While both case studies employ the same methodology
to assess risks, we present them in different formats to emphasize
the versatility of our methodology rather than adhering to a rigid
structure. It is beyond the scope of the book to consider all the
potential ways of partnership between a DAO and financial services
firms; the two case studies assume the DAOs are potential brokerage
and payment clients, respectively.

6.1 MakerDAO

6.1.1 *About the DAO*

MakerDAO is built on the Ethereum blockchain. It operates the Maker Protocol, which enables the creation of DAI, a stablecoin pegged to the US dollar.

The critical components of MakerDAO include the following:

(1) **The stablecoin (DAI)**: DAI is a stablecoin that aims to maintain a value of approximately USD 1. It achieves this stability through a combination of smart contracts and collateral backing, primarily in the form of ETH but more recently also in off-chain government-issued securities, such as US treasuries.

(2) **Collateralized Debt Positions (CDPs) and vaults**: With this, users can lock up collateral, for example, in the form of ETH and generate DAI against it. These CDPs are managed via smart contracts. Overcollateralization is a requirement. Collateral can be liquidated if the value of the position falls below a certain level.

(3) **Maker (MKR) token**: MKR is the governance token of the MakerDAO ecosystem. Holders of MKR have voting rights to participate in governance. They can vote on changing parameters, risk management strategies, and system upgrades.

At the time of writing, MakerDAO's DAI token is the 23rd largest cryptocurrency listed on coinmarketcap.com, with a market capitalization of over USD 5.3 billion.

For this case study, we assume that the DAO is a brokerage client. In this relationship, the broker acts as an agent for the DAO, assisting with purchasing and selling securities. No borrowing or lending activity is undertaken. The broker's revenue comes in the form of execution fees that the DAO client must pay. The impact assessment may differ if the DAO is engaged in a different capacity, for example, as a service provider to the financial institution.

6.1.2 *DAO accountability risk*

DAO accountability risk is the risk of not being able to clearly identify a representative responsible for a DAO and its members' actions.

6.1.2.1 *Impact*

When considering MakerDAO as a brokerage client, the accountability risk is high. For a financial institution, the implications of not knowing the identity of the individuals making the ultimate decisions in a client organization like MakerDAO and the possibility of them being rogue actors pose significant accountability risks. These risks may affect the institution's regulatory status and damage its reputation.

Impact rating: High (3).

6.1.2.2 *Probability*

A search for MakerDAO employees on LinkedIn's social network platform reveals 53 individuals, including the Founder, Rune Christensen. Core team members are not anonymous, reducing the probability of accountability risk-related incidents. A second data point affecting our probability rating for MakerDAO is the documentation of reference transactions with traditional financial services firms. Through intermediaries and relevant legal structures, MakerDAO has engaged Sygnum Bank, a fully licensed Swiss bank, to assist with purchasing several hundreds of millions worth of US Treasuries and corporate bonds.[1]

Probability rating: Low (1).

Overall accountability risk: Impact rating (3) × probability rating (1) = 3.

6.1.3 *DAO community risk*

DAO community risk is the risk of failing to attract, engage, and retain community members.

6.1.3.1 *Impact*

When assessing MakerDAO as a brokerage client, the community risk affecting the broker's operations or strategic objectives is low.

---

[1] https://www.coindesk.com/markets/2023/06/01/makerdao-paves-way-for-additional-128b-us-treasury-purchase (accessed on 6 June 2024).

If MakerDAO community members leave the DAO for a more attractive crypto stablecoin issuer, the broker would only lose fee income from a shrinking client.

Impact rating: Low (1).

6.1.3.2 *Probability*

The user base of MakerDAO's product, DAI, is well established, with a daily turnover reaching over USD 630 million at the time of writing. This high turnover suggests that the product's utility is evident and the community actively uses DAI. The total value locked (TVL) of over USD 5.3 billion demonstrates the strength of the DAO's community and engagement. The MakerDAO's DeFillama.com page further indicates that engagement from the developer community is relatively stable over time giving additional confidence.[2]

Probability rating: Low (1).

Overall community risk: Impact rating (1) × probability rating (1) = 1.

6.1.4 *DAO financial risk*

DAO financial risk is the risk that a DAO fails to meet its financial obligations due to the inappropriate level of diversification in its treasury portfolio.

6.1.4.1 *Impact*

The impact of financial risk on a brokerage company is low. MakerDAO could only account for the loss of fee income as no credit or market risk is involved in typical brokerage transactions.

Impact rating: Low (1).

---

[2]https://defillama.com/protocol/makerdao#information (accessed on 6 June 2024).

6.1.4.2 *Probability*

MakerDAO's Deepdao.io page reveals a concentrated portfolio of seven cryptocurrencies in MakerDAO's treasury portfolio.[3] Two stand out: MKR (the DAO's own token) with ca. 55% and UNI (the governance token of decentralized exchange Uniswap) with ca. 43%. The portfolio contains no significant stablecoin holdings. Because cryptocurrency markets are traditionally highly correlated, this treasury portfolio's financial risk is high.

Probability rating: High (3).

Overall financial risk: Impact rating (1) $\times$ probability rating (3) = 3.

6.1.5 *DAO governance risk*

DAO governance risk is the risk of a DAO's decision-making processes becoming dysfunctional.

6.1.5.1 *Impact*

If MakerDAO's governance fails to enable its community members to make decisions, the risk to a brokerage firm is low and unrelated to its strategic goals. Again, apart from losing the fee income, the impact is negligible.

Impact rating: Low (1).

6.1.5.2 *Probability*

We refer to Messari's governance module to analyze recent governance-related activity. At the time of writing, community members have raised 372 proposals since the launch of MakerDAO's governance in January 2021. The governance smart contract executed the last proposal on 6 May 2024, 4 days before we completed this section of our book. Hence, we can confirm there is recent governance

---

[3]https://deepdao.io/organization/c41f87df-35a6-4a37-82c4-62cd5a3a8c08/organi zation_data/finance (accessed on 6 June 2024).

activity. A random survey of a small number of proposals, however, reveals a high concentration of voting power among a few decision makers, raising concerns about the platform's decentralization, which may increase governance risk. An earlier study of MakerDAO's governance confirms these survey results (Sun *et al.*, 2024).

Probability rating: Low (1).

Overall governance risk: Impact rating (1) × probability rating (1) = 1.

6.1.6 *DAO operational risk*

DAO operational risk is the risk of loss resulting from inadequate or failed processes, people, and systems or from external events.

6.1.6.1 *Impact*

The breakdown of other processes, systems, or people or the severe effect of external events on a DAO's operation would, again, only affect the ability of the broker to keep trading with the DAO but no other impact.

Impact rating: Low (1).

6.1.6.2 *Probability*

The emergent business model of MakerDAO (decentralized money), the lack of regulatory standards, and the adversarial cryptographic environment in which MakerDAO operates, where hackers constantly attempt to extract value from smart contracts, make the likelihood of operational risk of MakerDAO high.

Probability rating: High (3).

Overall operational risk: Impact rating (1) × probability rating (3) = 3.

6.1.7 *DAO technology risk*

DAO technology risk is a type of DAO operational risk resulting from blockchain and related infrastructure outages or malfunctions.

6.1.7.1 *Impact*

The potential loss of a brokerage client due to technical risks resulting from a DAO operating on a public blockchain can ultimately only impact the broker's fee income. Unless the DAO client is very large, the impact here is low.

Impact rating: Low (1).

6.1.7.2 *Probability*

To assess the probability of DAO technology risk, we use Chapter 2's characteristics of smart contract platforms. MakerDAO uses the Ethereum smart contract platform. Due to its extensive network, the Ethereum platform is reasonably secure. It is not designed to be natively scalable, which limits the transaction throughput. The low throughput is less of a concern for a brokerage firm engaging with a DAO. While Ethereum is stable and only had a few outages or malfunctions over extended periods, the platform suffers from substantial gas price fluctuations, making it hard for users to estimate its operating costs. This can have an impact on the DAO's profitability. Ethereum is Turing-complete, increasing the risks associated with logic in programming (smart contract risk); this could lead to problems with the MakerDAO smart contracts and halt its operation. Ethereum's reputation among financial institutions is acceptable — many use it as a sandbox to experiment with blockchains. Ethereum operates on the Proof-of-Stake (PoS) consensus mechanism, which consumes much less energy than its Proof-of-Work (PoW)-based peers. In its current (Dencun) version, Ethereum does not support privacy-preserving features, making it less suitable for financial services applications that need to comply with personal data protection laws. The lack of a governance module also increases the risk of issues relating to good governance.

Probability rating: High (3).

Overall technology risk: Impact rating (1) × probability rating (3) = 3.

6.1.8 *One way to decide*

Now, we aggregate the individual risk category scores of the DAO. To do so, we need to make assumptions on the weight of each of the six risk categories. For the MakerDAO example, we assume that all risks are equally weighted to simplify the explanation. In practice, each institution will approach the weighting process according to its own internal risk management guidelines.

Remember

$$\Pi\,\text{DAOrisk} \approx \sum a\text{Ar} + b\text{Cr} + c\text{Fr} + d\text{Gr} + e\text{Or} + f\text{Tr},$$

where Ar denotes the accountability risk score, Cr the community risk score, Fr the financial risk score, Gr the governance risk score, Or the operational risk score, Tr the technology risk score, and Σa, b, c, d, e, $f \equiv 1$ expresses the weights financial institutions can assign according to their risk appetite.

If we calculate the DAO risk score for this MakerDAO, we get

$$2.34 \approx \sum 0.167 * 3 + 0.167 * 1 + 0.167 * 3 + 0.167 * 1$$
$$+ 0.167 * 3 + 0.167 * 3.$$

For this case study, the risk score is 2.34 on a scale of 1–9. The risk of interacting with MakerDAO for a brokerage firm with the above illustrative inputs is low to medium. This relatively low score can be attributed to the low impact scores. The impact is low because of the fee-based business model of a brokerage firm. If the risk appetite of the broker is in line with this result, the executive in charge may decide to go ahead and interact with the DAO. Please note that this risk assessment is a simplified version of what a real firm would have to do to make the decision. It is certainly not an endorsement or a recommendation for MakerDAO.

6.2 KlimaDAO

6.2.1 *About the DAO*

KlimaDAO is positioning itself as a DAO fighting climate change using Web3 technology. It does so by running a blockchain-based trading platform for the carbon market. The carbon market suffers from opacity, and KlimaDAO's mission is to improve its transparency, efficiency, and accessibility and to enable individuals and organizations to participate effectively in it. The protocol Klima is built on the Polygon blockchain. KlimaDAO's native token is $KLIMA. Each KLIMA token issued is backed by at least one ton of carbon offsets in the KlimaDAO treasury in the form of Base Carbon Tonne (BCT).[4] A BCT is a tokenized carbon credit that represents one metric ton of carbon dioxide equivalent (CO_2e) that has been removed or prevented from entering the atmosphere. Carbon offsets are verified and converted into digital tokens called Base Carbon Tonnes (BCTs) by Toucan, the carbon credit marketplace. The Toucan Carbon Bridge takes a verified carbon offset from a physical world registry, retires it from existence, and creates one BCT in its place. This process brings carbon offsets from the physical world to a public blockchain.

The impact on the financial institution will vary depending on the type of relationship it has with the DAO. For this case study discussion, we assume that the KlimaDAO is a cash management client of a bank. In this relationship, the bank assists with payment services with KlimaDAO's off-chain counterparties. No borrowing or lending activity is undertaken. The bank's sources of revenue are from account and transaction fees.

6.2.2 *DAO accountability risk*

DAO accountability risk is the risk of not being able to clearly identify a representative responsible for DAO and its members' actions.

When KlimaDAO was first created in 2021, its core team members kept their physical identities private and individuals were known only by their pseudonyms (e.g. Archimedes, Atmosfearful, Cujo, Dionysus). In these early stages, KlimaDAO's accountability risk was high. However, over time, some of the core members have revealed

---

[4]https://docs.klimadao.finance/economics/operational-mechanics/intrinsic-value (accessed on 13 May 2024).

their identities (e.g. Co-Founder Chaz Schmidt on LinkedIn). It is also possible to establish the physical world identities of their key team members as they often speak at high-profile crypto events in person. Additionally, to conduct business with off-chain carbon credit counterparties or financial institutions, the founders provide physical world identities bilaterally. In December 2023, the DAO voted to incorporate a Klima Foundation in the Cayman Islands to facilitate KYC and KYB requirements of their counterparties.[5] The Klima Foundation is led by a president and has a board of directors. The probability of accountability-related issues with the DAO has decreased since the decision to incorporate it as a Foundation. When considering KlimaDAO as a cash management client, there is still residual accountability risk because it is not possible to know all identities of individuals contributing to the governance process by voting with their governance tokens.

Impact rating: High (3).

Probability rating: Medium (2).

Overall accountability risk: Impact rating (3) × probability rating (2) = 6.

6.2.3 *DAO community risk*

DAO community risk is the risk of failing to attract, engage, and retain community members.

When doing research on a DAO, it is often useful to join their Discord channel and speak to the community to find out about the latest developments as these are not always instantly reflected on their website. Going to a DAO's Discord to ask questions to the community will reveal how open, communicative, and active the community members are.

As of writing in May 2024, the KilmaDAO community is visibly active as evidenced by the frequency and recency of their proposals

---

[5]https://snapshot.org/#/klimadao.eth/proposal/0x350e2d9e8dc1041b02f2cce4f5 6f632382a922c1a72c6008f55c420ea44bf660 (accessed on 2 May 2024).

and voting.[6] Their Discord channel has over 30,000 members and there are regular and timely announcements from the core team, and much interaction between the members themselves can be observed. At its peak at launch, their Discord had over 60,000 members. Their X (formerly Twitter) account has nearly 68,000 followers. The Klima team is continually launching new initiatives. For example, on 25 April 2024, the KLIMA token was launched on Base, a new Ethereum Layer 2 blockchain developed by Coinbase. At its inception, the DAO enjoyed a surge in community members. There was a decrease in membership numbers that followed the extreme token price drop (which will be examined in more detail in Section 6.2.5). Regardless of the smaller community now, the DAO can engage its members. When assessing KlimaDAO as a cash management client, the community risk affecting the bank's operations is low. If KlimaDAO fails to retain its community members, the bank will simply lose the DAO as a cash management client with no adverse impact on the bank's operations or strategy other than the lack of projected account and transaction fee income.

Impact rating: Low (1).

Probability rating: Medium (2).

Overall community risk: Impact rating (1) $\times$ probability rating (2) = 2.

6.2.4 *DAO financial risk*

DAO financial risk is the risk that a DAO fails to meet its financial obligations due to the inappropriate level of diversification in its treasury portfolio.

Typically, a DAO's treasury wallet address is shared on its website and Discord. KlimaDAO has two multi-sig wallets: one for operations

---

[6]https://deepdao.io/organization/b2847d58-24e9-49a2-a8bf-f9d582c8b24f/organization_data/governance (accessed on 3 May 2024).

and one for treasury.[7,8] The operations wallet is used to pay contributors and expenses. At less than USD 500,000, it appears small. The treasury wallet is a smart contract which programmatically holds assets that back KLIMA tokens. The treasury attracted significant funds at launch but has since tapered off and currently has a size of about USD 13 million. About 90% of the treasury is in BCT. This overweight exposure to BCT is in line with KlimaDAO's mission to scale environmental commodity markets using blockchain and DeFi. The treasury wallet is one of Klima's main tools and as such, it is strategically allocated to environmental commodities. Carbon is currently the main environmental commodity in a new and immature market. The impact of the financial risk of KlimaDAO as a payment client for a financial institution is low. The DAO's strategy of holding mostly carbon credits results in a highly concentrated treasury portfolio.

Early on, KlimaDAO faced controversy due to its tokenomics design. The minting and distribution of KLIMA tokens was highly inflationary, and its annual percentage yields (APYs) were as high as 30,000% in the first year. However, this unsustainable model led to the dilution of $KLIMA's value, causing the token price to plummet from $1,980 in October 2021 to $2.50 in May 2024.

Impact rating: Low (1).

Probability rating: High (3).

Overall financial risk: Impact rating (1) $\times$ probability rating (3) = 3.

6.2.5 *DAO governance risk*

DAO governance risk is the risk of a DAO's decision-making processes becoming dysfunctional.

---

[7]https://etherscan.io/address/0x7Dd4f0B986F032A44F913BF92c9e8b7c17D77a
D7#multichain-portfolio (accessed on 8 May 2024).
[8]https://polygonscan.com/address/0x65a5076c0ba74e5f3e069995dc3dab9d197d
995c (accessed on 8 May 2024).

If KlimaDAO's governance fails to enable its community members to make decisions, the impact on the bank is low, as the latter's loss is in transaction fee income from KlimaDAO. KlimaDAO's degree of decentralization is currently relatively low. The core team holds significantly large amounts of KLIMA governance tokens, allowing them to control decision-making. The multi-sig wallet access to protocol code and treasury gives them considerable power which can increase governance risk (Jirasek, 2023).

Impact rating: Low (1).

Probability rating: High (3).

Overall governance risk: Impact rating (1) × probability rating (3) = 3.

6.2.6 *DAO operational risk*

DAO operational risk is the risk of loss resulting from inadequate or failed processes, people, and systems or from external events.

KlimaDAO brings off-chain carbon credits to the blockchain by tokenizing them. As such, there are operational issues involved in the off-chain/on-chain translation process. For example, in the carbon credit industry, there are a few dominant carbon credit certification bodies including Verra and Gold Standard. When Klima was first launched in 2021, it quickly accumulated over 20 million tons of Verra carbon credits. However, in 2022, Verra blocked the process and Klima had to look for alternative registries to source carbon credits.[9]

Greenwashing is the practice of making misleading or false claims about the environmental benefits of a product or service to make it appear more environmentally friendly and compliant than they actually are. Governments and regulators around the world are increasingly recognizing the problem of greenwashing and taking various steps to combat it through guidelines, regulations, fines,

---

[9]https://verra.org/verra-addresses-crypto-instruments-and-tokens/ (accessed on 10 May 2024).

and penalties. Quality and legitimacy of carbon credits can vary greatly, and the carbon credit market is susceptible to greenwashing. KlimaDAO faces the risk of being associated with greenwashing due to the potential for low-quality or fraudulent carbon credits to be tokenized and traded on its platform. If the carbon credits backed by BCTs are not properly vetted or do not represent genuine, additional, and permanent carbon emission reductions, KlimaDAO could be seen as enabling the sale and circulation of dubious offsets. This is a source of operational risk.

Impact rating: High (3).

Probability rating: High (3).

Overall operational risk: Impact rating (9) $\times$ probability rating (3) = 9.

6.2.7 *DAO technology risk*

DAO technology risk is a type of DAO operational risk resulting from blockchain and related infrastructure outages or malfunctions.

The potential loss of a payment client due to technical risks resulting from a DAO operating on a public blockchain can ultimately only impact the bank's transaction fee income. Unless the DAO client is very large, the impact here is low.

KlimaDAO operates on Polygon, a Layer 2 network on Ethereum, and as such bears somewhat higher security-related risks. Polygon allows for faster transactions than Ethereum, making it more scalable. The low number of validators of the network increases centralization. Polygon does offer low and predictable fees as an L2 network. Since Polygon is a Layer 2 on Ethereum, any issues or setbacks faced by Ethereum could indirectly impact Polygon. Additionally, Polygon historically had outages affecting DApps running on it. Polygon is Turing-complete, increasing the risks associated with logic in programming (smart contract risk); this could lead to problems with the KlimaDAO smart contracts and halt its operation. Despite the large marketing budgets and professional appearance, Polygon's reputation has suffered due to the low number of validating nodes. Polygon is starting to offer privacy-preserving features through Polygon Miden, which is positive.[10]

Impact rating: Low (1).

Probability rating: Medium (3).

Overall technology risk: Impact rating (1) × probability rating (3) = 3.

6.2.8 *One way to decide*

Now, we aggregate the individual risk category scores of a DAO. To do so, we need to make assumptions on the weight of each of the six risk categories. For the KlimaDAO example, we assume that all risks are equally weighted to simplify the explanation. In practice, each institution will approach the weighting process according to its own internal risk management guidelines.

Remember

$$\Pi\, \mathrm{DAOrisk} \approx \sum a\mathrm{Ar} + b\mathrm{Cr} + c\mathrm{Fr} + d\mathrm{Gr} + e\mathrm{Or} + f\mathrm{Tr},$$

where Ar denotes the accountability risk score, Cr the community risk score, Fr the financial risk score, Gr the governance risk score, Or the operational risk score, Tr the technology risk score, and Σa, b, c, d, e, $f \equiv 1$ expresses the weights financial institutions can assign according to their risk appetite.

If we calculate the DAO risk score for KlimaDAO we get

$$4.34 \approx \sum 0.167 * 6 + 0.167 * 2 + 0.167 * 3 + 0.167 * 3$$

$$+ 0.167 * 9 + 0.167 * 3.$$

For this case study, the risk score is 4.34 on a scale of 1–9. The risk to a bank considering interaction with KlimaDAO as a cash management client with the above illustrative inputs is low to medium. If the risk appetite of the bank is in line with this, the executive in charge may decide to go ahead and interact with the DAO.

---

[10]https://polygon.technology/blog/privacy-a-fundamental-right-and-a-practical-necessity (accessed on 13 May 2024).

Please note that this risk assessment is a simplified version of what a real firm would have to do to make the decision. It is certainly not an endorsement or a recommendation of KlimaDAO.

References

Jirasek, M., 2023. Klima DAO: A Crypto Answer to Carbon Markets. *Journal of Organization Design.* https://link.springer.com/article/10.1007/s41469-023-00146-w.

Sun, X., Stasinkis, C., and Sermpinis, G., 2024. Decentralization Illusion in Decentralized Finance: Evidence from Tokenized Voting in MakerDAO Polls. *Journal of Financial Stability.* https://www.sciencedirect.com/science/article/pii/S1572308924000718.

PART 3

Chapter 7

Interviews

Abstract

This chapter presents four interviews with experts, offering unique perspectives on the challenges and opportunities of decentralized autonomous organizations (DAOs). Hagen Rooke, a financial regulatory and FinTech lawyer, discusses the legal aspects of DAOs, including the relationship between operating companies and DAOs, the enforceability of smart contracts, and the liabilities of DAO members. Sharon Paul, Co-Founder and CEO of Headquarters (HQ.xyz), explains how her company helps DAOs manage their treasury and financial operations. Professor Sinclair Davidson, from the RMIT Blockchain Innovation Hub, shares his research on applying existing economic and management theories to understand DAOs and identifies pressing gaps in DAO research. Bill Laboon, Director of Education and Governance Initiatives at Web3 Foundation, introduces Polkadot's value proposition, its evolution, and the challenges Polkadot DAO faces when interacting with traditional financial institutions.

7.1 Legal perspective: Hagen Rooke, Reed Smith

1. *Please introduce yourself to our readers.*

I'm Hagen Rooke, a financial regulatory and FinTech lawyer at Reed Smith based in Singapore. My practice focuses on regulatory advisory and commercial contractual work for financial institutions and corporates, ranging from banks and fund managers to payment firms, crypto exchanges, and commodity traders. The use of new technologies, including digital and Web3 offerings, has always been a cornerstone of my practice. I am qualified to practice Singapore law and English law, but many of the projects I advise on are multijurisdictional or cross-border in nature.

2. *Tell us about the work you do with DAOs directly or indirectly.*

We advise on a range of different matters involving DAOs. Our client is usually the developer team that is setting up a DAO. There is a sizeable global community of DAO developers, many of whom operate in the decentralized finance (DeFi) space and are located in centers, such as Singapore, Hong Kong, Dubai, or London. Being located in these centers gives the developers touchpoints with peers and easier access to capital and infrastructure.

It is usually advisable for these developer teams to set up an operating entity in the location where they are based. Separately, these developers will typically want to set up a decentralized structure in an offshore location such as the British Virgin Islands (BVI) or the Cayman Islands to support their DAO. From a legal perspective, our task is often to find a structure that will allow for insulation of risks that can arise in connection with operating a DAO while still enabling the DAO to operate in a decentralized manner. These objectives are not always easily reconciled, but that's generally what we do. We help the developer teams navigate regulatory, contractual, operational, and litigation risks, and we try to do this with the most efficient setup possible.

3. *What is the relationship between an operating company and a DAO? What are their respective responsibilities?*

An operating company will usually be set up in the onshore location where the developer team is predominantly located, and the company will do several things to support the development and operation of a DAO. For example, it will often hold the IP that the project is developing. If the developer team is looking to launch a DAO, generally this may involve developing IP like copyright in relation to the coding of the blockchain-based protocol underpinning the DAO or the creation of any front-end user applications that facilitate user access to the DAO. There might also be branding and logos that are registered as trademarks. These are all forms of IP that may be housed in that operating company. The operating company will also employ or appoint employees or contractors who support the development of the DAO. Often, the company will also undertake equity fundraising activities.

Essentially therefore, the onshore operating company carries out all the centralized activities. Structurally, these centralized activities will be segregated from the decentralized DAO operations that occur offshore. To support the decentralized operations, an offshore entity that will function as a "legal wrapper" for the DAO will usually be established in a favorable jurisdiction. The BVI and the Cayman Islands have traditionally been jurisdictions of choice for many DAO projects, but as these jurisdictions have become more regulated over time, there has been some movement to locations such as Seychelles or Panama that are not yet as progressed in their rollout of regulation.

As a DAO needs to function in a decentralized manner, the choice of entity to house the DAO's operations must be consistent with decentralization. Commonly, projects set up a foundation, which is a very flexible form of an entity. Importantly, a foundation is ownerless (foundations are sometimes referred to as "orphan entities"), so there won't be any shareholders. This fits in well with the ethos of decentralization because the foundation only has a governing body with directors who formalize the decisions that are made collectively by the DAO user community. The absence of any ultimate beneficial ownership and the possibility of appointing directors who are separate from those of the onshore operating company means that the foundation — and with it, the DAO — can be functionally segregated from the onshore operations and does not sit within the same group structure as the onshore company.

The question, then, is how the offshore entity connects with the onshore operating entity. Most often, there is a service agreement between the onshore operating entity and the offshore entity. Under that service agreement, the onshore entity provides technical and operational support to the offshore entity. In return for the support, the DAO will pay a fee to the operating entity for the services.

The payment from the DAO (usually in cryptocurrency) comes out of its treasury, which in turn is the revenue earned via the DAO operations. The DAO will need some form of operational support on an ongoing basis even if it is self-executing and smart contract-based. Initially in particular, before the DAO has gained a critical degree of community adoption and has become decentralized, it will need to be supported by the operating company. So, the service arrangement between the onshore company and the offshore entity allows for operational support but also repatriation of value generated by the DAO operations.

4. Smart contracts are an intrinsic part of DAOs. In essence, smart contracts are computer programs and not legal contracts. Can you share with us your experiences about the enforceability of smart contracts in a court of law?

There are semantic challenges involved in understanding smart contracts. There is also a legitimate question around the role of smart contracts in legal agreements. The thing with smart contracts is they are really just pieces of code. They auto-execute: If condition X is met, then consequence Y will follow. Now, that in itself can be helpful when you're trying to devise a system that allows for, for example, settlement finality or immutability because whether the conditions are met will be verified on the blockchain before a smart contract auto-executes. But all of that happens just in the technological universe. None of it has any legal relevance until you ascribe legal relevance to it, either because a government draws up a law and says "we will recognize that smart contract-executed transactions are legally enforceable contracts," or you as a matter of private law draw up a contract with your counterparty and say "as a matter of contract, we will recognize that transactions executed by smart contract will be recognized as valid and binding by us." Here, I am distinguishing between the legal contract and the piece of code. I think for the non-legal community, the biggest challenge is always to understand that smart contracts are not actually legal constructs until the point where a law or a legal contract says so.

If you take DAOs in their most pure, archetypal form, they don't have any legal agreement or entity structure that underpins them. We have various clients who have approached us and said "we have absolutely no legal architecture at all — no legal entities, no contracts, nothing. Please help us to formalize this structure." We then help these developers after they have already created a DAO by setting up a legal wrapper for the DAO and putting in place agreements between the different entities and individuals involved in the structure. The point is, again, that a DAO operating on the basis of smart contracts (essentially, pieces of code) will only have rudimentary legal recognition until you give it some more carefully structured legal underpinning.

However, with DeFi now having come of age, lots of DAOs actually have terms and conditions. If we use the examples of an automated market maker or a lending protocol, the terms and conditions set out exactly when you will be entering into a legally binding transaction. Some terms and conditions are very specific as to the transactions that are carried out through a DAO and what a user's rights and obligations are.

5. *What are the liabilities for a DAO member who is simply a smallholder of the governance token?*

Generally, if you're a user, you're a participant in the governance of a DAO. Your baseline expectation will be that you shouldn't be held liable for the actions of the DAO because you do not have sole discretion or authority to make decisions for the DAO — it is a collective governance process involving the user community as a whole. For most DAOs, there is a democratic process where at least a majority of participants have to vote on a proposal for it to be implemented. But protecting users from liability can be complicated where there is no legal infrastructure to support the DAO. In some cases, we have seen DAOs that don't have any kind of legal wrapper, for example, no foundation was set up to support them. They don't have any other kind of company or trust to support them, and consequently, there will be no terms and conditions with users of the DAO. The question then arises as to what the legal classification of the DAO activities actually is. There have been court decisions handed down in the US to the effect that if a group of persons engages in some kind of common enterprise and co-runs a DAO business, this amounts to a general partnership. In a general partnership, participants have joint unlimited liability for the activities that are being undertaken. To avoid this situation, a business will often be set up as a company or other entity for which the co-owners or stakeholders only have limited liability and where specific functionaries (such as directors) have well-defined duties. This allows for individual participants in the arrangement to be protected from liability for the business activities undertaken, which in legal circles we call the "corporate veil," and the corporate veil will only be pierced in very limited and exceptional instances. This is a key reason why we recommend creating a legal wrapper like a foundation or other entity for a DAO.

6. If someone wants to be an active member of a DAO, as a lawyer, what points would you ask them to consider?

For all the reasons I raised in Question 5, I suggest first looking at whether the DAO has any terms and conditions and whether it has any legal structure to support it. I recognize that it can sound like a contradiction to have a DAO and at the same time, to say it needs a legal structure. We have clients who are DAO developers and who subscribe to an ethos of decentralization. And they have a grassroots approach of wanting to democratize finance, which incidentally, I am also very sympathetic to. But being lawyers, our task is to insulate clients from risk, and we do that by introducing legal structures and a degree of centralization and trusted intermediation. So, to a user of a DAO, I would say: Look at the terms and conditions of the DAO, and whether the DAO has legal entities supporting it, because you don't want to be in a situation where you end up being a partner in a general partnership with unlimited liability for what the DAO is doing. Look at what the terms and conditions say. What are your rights and obligations if something adverse were to happen? What kind of recourse do you have if your tokens end up being locked up in the DAO and you cannot retrieve them? Do you know who you would be able to make a claim against? These are the things I would advise a DAO user to consider.

Of course, as a DAO user, you won't really have much ability to negotiate, or to change the legal position and say "this isn't sufficient, I want to have additional rights against the DAO." In the event of a claim or dispute, a user may be able to invoke the dispute resolution process in the DAO terms and conditions, if existent. This being the case, if there is a claim against a DAO or its developer team (e.g. if individuals with signing rights over smart contracts containing users' tokens orchestrate a "rug pull"), our experience is that being able to trace the assets, let alone recover them via court proceedings or arbitration can be quite difficult. So, we would recommend that alongside due diligence from a legal perspective, users also undertake due diligence on the underlying developers. Are they legitimate? Do they have a good track record? Is the team known in the industry and perceived as trustworthy? Even if you may not get the answer to all of those questions, you should inquire.

7. If a banker or financial services professional wants to onboard a DAO as a client, what are the requisite steps to make it happen?

I think there are a number of considerations here. Having a bank account is critical if a DAO is looking to integrate conversions between cryptocurrency and fiat currency (i.e. "on-ramps" or "off-ramps") or wishes to raise funds or pay personnel or suppliers in fiat currency. Generally speaking, however, DAO projects have difficulty opening bank accounts, even if they have a formalized legal structure since banks are traditionally risk-averse and associate money-laundering and terrorism-financing risks with crypto businesses. To the extent a bank account is opened, this will typically be maintained by the onshore operating company, partly because this company will be a software development or technology company which has a substantive business and whose activities are one degree removed from the DAO operations.

Even if financial institutions were in principle willing to offer services directly to DAOs, as a gating consideration and for onboarding purposes, they would focus on whether there are controllers, owners, or sponsors who are principally responsible for the DAO. If it is a genuine DAO that has reached a high degree of decentralization, then there may not actually be any person that you can classify as a controller or ultimate beneficial owner of the DAO. So, the first challenge would be for financial institutions to resign themselves to this reality and say "okay fine, there's no beneficial owner or other person pulling the strings here, but because it's a DAO, we can nonetheless get comfortable with onboarding it." I think that would require quite a novel approach to the way KYC is conducted. As a minimum, then, the financial institution would need to understand the source of funds it will receive from the DAO. Since it may not be practical to answer this question by looking through and identifying the users of the DAO, the financial institution may only be able to get satisfied if it knows the DAO itself is carrying out robust anti-money laundering (AML) checks. By analogy, in the traditional world, if you are a bank dealing with a fund manager or other regulated entity, you may not need to look through that entity's customers or investors when carrying out AML checks and enquiring into questions, such as the source of funds. A further point the financial institution would need to be comfortable with is that it can actually contract with the DAO — the DAO has to have a legal personality and must be capable of entering into an agreement with the financial institution, and the financial institution has to be satisfied that it has enforceable rights under the agreement.

Let's also not forget creditworthiness. If I am a financial institution, I will want to know that a person I'm contracting with (here, a DAO) is sufficiently solvent to meet its obligations. A DAO may have a treasury, but that doesn't necessarily mean that it has a balance sheet and profit and loss accounts. In fact, from an accounting perspective, the transactions of a DAO may not be booked to the entity which functions as the DAO's legal wrapper, and this may complicate the financial institution's risk assessment. This is one reason why the assessment of a DAO's creditworthiness may have to be technological and operational in nature, rather than legal. And this is why we often talk about moving from the rule of law to the rule of code; in the DeFi space, you're no longer fully relying on the law, you are trusting the code.

8. *If someone came to you and said excitedly "I want to start a DAO." As a lawyer, what questions would you ask them to consider?*

I will start with a question that is a bit tongue-in-cheek, before moving to the more determinative inquiries. The tongue-in-cheek question is: "Are you fully certain you need a DAO?" I say that simply because we have many clients who say they want to launch a DAO, but it then turns out that they don't really need a DAO, they actually just need an entity via which they can sell tokens, or they want to set up a centralized trading platform. So, the more determinative question is: "Do you need an arrangement that is decentralized, to support a platform that is governed only by its community of users?" If the answer is yes, then you probably need a DAO.

Then you get into the more serious structuring questions, such as "Where are your people?" By which I mean: Where are your developers, your founders, and the team that is going to provide operational support to the DAO? This will determine, for example, where you set up your onshore operating company, and then where you end up holding your IP. Another question is: "Where are the users of the DAO predominantly going to be located? Are you aiming for a particular geography?" Because again, that might influence the structure you choose. There are different regulatory frameworks that are at different stages of maturity in different parts of the world, and these have to be navigated carefully, taking into account of the location of DAO users.

A further question is: "What kind of IP do you think you will be generating? Are you putting a lot of proprietary developmental work into this DAO? Or are you just using an open-source model?" If you are using open-source code, then you may not be generating proprietary IP requiring protection. If you are generating such IP, however, then you should think about how you protect it. We generally recommend that the IP sits in the operating company, but sometimes you can also set up a separate company to ring-fence the IP to reduce the risk of litigation against the operating company, resulting in enforcement against valuable IP assets.

The types of IP we see DAO developers generate include names, logos, and brands (which may be possible to protect via processes like trademark registration) as well as code and applications that may be protected by copyright. The challenge with copyright is that it is a form of IP that comes into existence but is not registered. It is therefore advisable to gather evidence of this IP having been generated, and a lot of our advice revolves around how to document the development process.

9. Within the current regulatory regime, what are the best options for a DAO to be legally compliant?

This question comes up a lot. The projects we speak to that want to set up a DAO clearly want to be legally compliant because that's why they're talking to their lawyers. If the DAO engages in DeFi activities, then the key question is whether this involves the DAO itself or its onshore developer team engaging in regulated financial activities; determining the position often requires a multijurisdictional analysis.

If the DAO is not involved in DeFi, then the financial regulatory element falls away, and there is less that is required for legal compliance. Interestingly in Singapore, there are quite a few DAOs that do not engage in DeFi but are involved in other activities, such as making grants to developer companies to support the buildout of on-chain ecosystems. These Singapore-based DAOs often use a company limited by guarantee as their legal wrapper; this is commonly referred to as a "Singapore foundation," although that is a misnomer. Generally, these entities are easy to set up, but compliance questions may arise in relation to the charitable status of the entity and its taxation.

9a. What are the differences between a foundation set up in Singapore and other jurisdictions? Which entity issues the governance token?

Conceptually, a Singapore "foundation" (actually, a company limited by guarantee, as explained in the previous question) and foundations set up in other jurisdictions are similar. However, they tend to be used in different ways, depending on the flexibility afforded to the entity under applicable company law and the permissibility of the regulatory framework. Singapore has historically been a choice of domicile for foundations due to a perception that Singapore is progressive and crypto-friendly; this has now given way to a more cautious approach due to the extensive regulatory framework that has been introduced in Singapore (and which continues to be phased in incrementally) to govern crypto-related activities. Consequently, DAO projects are no longer using Singapore as frequently as a place of domicile for their DAO legal wrapper, especially if the DAO engages in DeFi activities.

In Switzerland, foundations have afforded much flexibility to projects because they do everything from issuing the governance token to being the operating company and supporting the protocol. But outside of Switzerland, we find this combination of functions in a single entity to be very rare. What we see most often is a foundation or trust (frequently in the Cayman Islands) that supports the protocol operations, combined with a BVI subsidiary that can issue tokens (as the regulatory framework in the BVI is viewed as conducive to certain types of token issuance activity). Generally, the BVI company will conduct an initial private or public sale of tokens once a "token generation event" occurs (e.g. the project reaches a defined milestone in revenue generation or development). Proceeds raised by the BVI company flow up to the foundation, where they are held in the DAO treasury. The foundation may pay those proceeds to the onshore company under its service arrangement with that company.

10. *DAOs are fundamentally different from existing organizations. If you were given the power to pass and implement new DAO-friendly regulations, what would be on your wish list?*

This is a tricky question. On the one hand, it would be nice to have DAO regulations that facilitate DAO activities. On the other hand, the concept of regulation is quite antithetical to DAOs because the whole purpose is that they're supposed to operate in an institutional vacuum where there is no authority, government layer, or regulation that circumscribes the DAO's activities. So, I think coming up with regulations that are well-suited is difficult. It has been attempted before, for example, in Wyoming, where I believe the DAO framework received a muted reaction from the community. Ultimately, DAOs want flexibility and freedom to operate rather than a framework that reintroduces elements of centralized accountability. In terms of entity setup, I think DAOs actually operate pretty well in the context they commonly operate in today, using a dual onshore and offshore structure. It is also becoming increasingly apparent that existing regulatory frameworks for centralized activities may be applied to DAO activities, given that decentralization of DAOs tends to be imperfect and a control relationship can often be imputed to identifiable persons in DAO structures.

For those DAOs that are genuinely decentralized, however, the question becomes who should be regulated, because you can't really regulate the DAO itself since it is decentralized. Regulating the users seems like an unlikely route. Do you then regulate the developer company? What if the developers created the DAO a while ago and the DAO has since become entirely autonomous? Should DAOs be subject to regulatory audits before they are launched and their operation is handed over to community governance? These are some of the questions the legal and regulatory community is currently grappling with and which remain unresolved.

11. *What do you think is the future of DAOs?*

As legal advisors with a specialization in this area, we are really at the forefront of market developments. We get to see when there is a spike in interest and when the interest tails off again. Back in 2021 and 2022, DAOs were all the rage and we had a lot of DAO developer clients that were looking to go to market. While there continue to be new DAO projects today, I feel some of the momentum has tapered off, possibly because of the realization that DAO structures will eventually be brought into the scope of regulation in most jurisdictions. So, the question is: Will the ethos of decentralization ultimately prevail or will the gravitational force of centralization prompt us to increasingly revert to our trusted intermediaries? My sense is that technology that was pioneered in the DAO space — such as smart contracts and blockchain-based immutability — will be appropriated by the financial services sector over time, given the efficiencies it can help generate (e.g. less capital-intensive and operationally cumbersome trading, clearing, and settlement processes, and fewer participants in the value chain). It therefore seems likely that decentralized technology will cement its role in financial services, but it will look and feel different from the decentralization, which the grassroots DAO movement originally aspired to.

7.2 Service provider perspective: Sharon Paul, HQ.xyz

1. *Please introduce yourself and your team to our readers.*

I am Sharon Paul, Co-Founder and CEO of Headquarters (HQ.xyz), the finance back-office stack for Web3 firms and funds. Prior to Headquarters, I was Head of Payments at Fazz.com, a Southeast Asian FinTech group, and was a founding member of StraitsX, the leading stablecoin issuer for Southeast-Asian markets. The tokenizing of local currencies entailed bridging the traditional banking and payment rails with the stablecoin's smart contract, as well as engaging with local regulators to ensure that it complied with existing payment regulations. Beyond this, I seek to actively bridge the Web2 and Web3 FinTech industries and was recently appointed as a Web3.0 Sub-committee member in the Singapore FinTech Association (SFA). At HQ, my team comprises professionals from data engineering, FinTech, as well as local merchant commerce space. While varied in our past experiences, we share a strong common interest in enabling the ease for businesses to adopt digital assets. The rest of my team are Sunny Singh, Co-Founder, and Alex Teo, COO.

2. *Why have you started HQ.xyz, and why now?*

My Co-Founder, Sunny, and I started HQ to enable fellow business owners and operators to adopt digital assets with confidence. As with most founding stories, it takes serendipity for a startup to be born. It was great timing, both of us shared the desire to improve business adoption of digital assets while having accumulated complementary experiences: Sunny's expertise in data engineering, mine in FinTech, and tokenized assets. We met during 2017's crypto bull-run. Prior to and since then, we both built up our careers in early-stage ventures. Through these, we experienced first-hand the level of operational excellence needed for ventures to scale well. As Web3 emerged again from 2020 onward, in my previous role of leading payments and stablecoin initiatives, I witnessed the haphazard back-office that was behind some of these projects. It was serendipitous that Sunny also spotted the same issue then. In 2022, poor FinOps practices in Web3 took the spotlight when a few renowned industry players had very poor financial governance, pulling down the entire industry with them. As Web3 enters a more mature phase, it is apparent that businesses adopting and offering digital assets will have to significantly improve their back-office — so as to keep up with the demands of regulatory, consumer, and industry expectations.

3. *What does HQ.xyz do for DAOs?*

We help DAOs level up their operational excellence in managing their treasury and focus on scaling the DAO's mission.

Giving visibility and accountability over their finances, i.e. aggregated view of treasury and financial reporting, HQ provides DAOs with a real-time view of their treasury, be it in various digital assets (tokens, NFTs, stablecoins) or fiat. A DAO simply needs to import the addresses of their self-custodial wallets or to login via their custodial accounts, and HQ will automatically perform the bookkeeping of the transactions in a human-readable manner. This facilitates ease of understanding the FinOps context of the transaction, as well as having the spot and historical balance view of the assets. Most importantly, HQ also enables easy integration with accounting software such as QuickBooks and Xero. This makes it easy for DAOs to adopt best practices in financial accountability, whereby a DAO can easily produce financial statements as a regular company can do today.

Enabling fuss-free payments based on tokens or fiat DAOs today exists in a world that is still in transition between fiat and tokenized assets. It is common for DAOs to have a mix of expenses in fiat or cryptocurrencies and stablecoins. With HQ, DAOs can receive or make payments easily in either form. As the industry matures, the expectation for strong compliance practices, such as travel rule for transactions, may become the norm. HQ is integrated with various KYC providers to enable this as an option if needed.

4. *What challenges do you face at the intersection of the world of business as we know it and the decentralized one?*

A core challenge is that participants in the decentralized economy adopt very different treasury options compared to those of the mainstream marketplace. In today's marketplace, newer FinTechs are typically layers built above local banking players. In other words, the technology for holding assets and settling payments is primarily built on top of traditional banking infrastructure, such as the international SWIFT, United States' ACH, India's UPI, or Singapore's FAST network. This is in stark contrast to that of DeFi, where self-custodial wallets are built on top of public blockchains, and public blockchains, such as Ethereum, also act as their own primary settlement network. The challenge lies in providing users with a holistic and seamless experience that traverses both traditional and DeFi. A second challenge lies in the different accounting treatments between fiat and tokenized assets. Even if one were to transact in stablecoin, the differences in accounting treatment can sometimes be a hassle for businesses. Hence, this discourages experimentation by traditional businesses that might otherwise benefit from adopting digital assets in their business models or as payment options. Hence, there are multiple technological and regulatory hurdles in the way of seamlessly bridging traditional financial technologies with that of a decentralized financial system built on public blockchains.

5. Can you share your thoughts on how your work relates explicitly to the title of our book, Decentralized Autonomous Organizations: How Finance can Interact with Blockchain-based DAOs?

Blockchain-based DAOs primarily operate on digital assets. This ranges from running their governance or utility incentives through their own tokens as well as utilizing tokenized assets such as stablecoins for their FinOps. Headquarters (HQ.xyz) is a finance back-office startup focused on the Web3 industry. It used to be contentious that DAOs should operate differently from regular companies. However, the global spotlight on poor financial governance of centralized players in Web3 has spilled over to DAOs. DAOs are now expected to adopt proper FinOps practice so as to have strong financial health and hence continuity of the DAO. Such FinOps practices include having a treasury that is regularly and properly accounted for. In addition, there has been a rise in jurisdictions (e.g. Abu Dhabi, Wyoming, the Marshall Islands) putting in place legal frameworks to recognize DAOs as a unique entity type. Abu Dhabi, in particular, has proposed rules that will require DAOs (or "DLT foundations") to maintain accounting records and have audited financial statements. HQ provides a full suite of finance back-office solutions for entities with digital assets. We fulfill this in two ways: (1) HQ Dashboard, a tool to automate payments and accounting of on-chain transactions and digital assets. With HQ Dashboard, teams can easily reconcile transactions in a human-readable manner as well as export into regular accounting tools, such as Xero, Quickbooks Online, and Netsuite. (2) HQ Concierge, an expert network of crypto-savvy financial services professionals who can be seconded to DAOs as fractional CFOs, finance controllers, and/or accountants. Common services include monthly management/community reports, annual tax filings, and treasury operations.

6. Let's think ahead. DAOs are ubiquitous in the world of collaboration and business. What changes compared to today?

In a world where DAOs are ubiquitous, it is highly likely that they would have learned the lessons of their predecessors and recognized that accountability and strong governance practices are also important elements of running a successful DAO. For instance, in the aftermath of the FTX crash, we saw some DAOs lose track of their finances and go under as a result. DAOs should still offer the promise of decentralization, transparency, and security, but what will change is that accountability is likely also become a core tenet of how DAOs operate. We envisage DAOs appointing members to oversee core treasury functions so as to manage runway and risks. DAOs will likely share best practices among themselves with regard to how to manage their financial operations.

7.3 Academic perspective: Prof. Dr. Sinclair Davidson, RMIT

1. *Please introduce yourself to our readers.*

I'm a Professor of Economics in the Blockchain Innovation Hub at RMIT University in Melbourne, Australia. I first got involved in Crypto in late 2015 when some colleagues and I started writing a paper on the economics of Ethereum. We quickly realized that this was a far bigger project than we had initially thought, and we ended up writing a paper that became the foundation of a new field of economics: institutional cryptoeconomics. Since then, we've just gone deeper and deeper into the Crypto rabbit hole. I've also spent a lot of time working with crypto startups advising them on their business models and token economics.

2. *What are your main research contributions to the understanding of DAOs?*

I apply the existing theories that economists and management academics have used to explain and understand existing organizational forms (especially the modern corporations) to DAOs. DAOs are not just "businesses on the internet." Although many people see them and think of them as being just that. Rather, DAOs are hybrid organizational forms that include aspects of markets, the modern firm, commons, and government. Each of those organizational forms has unique characteristics and governance mechanisms. My research attempts to unravel all those features and understand how they all fit together and function in a coherent manner.

3. *Could you tell us about the work of RMIT Blockchain Hub and the RMIT Docklands DAO?*

I am one of the three co-founders of the Blockchain Innovation Hub at RMIT University. We are the world's first social science, as opposed to computer science, unit that is dedicated to understanding how this new technology will impact both the economy and broader society. We are techno-optimists. We believe that this technology (and related technologies such as AI) will unambiguously improve the human condition, but it will be disruptive in the near future. Our role is to explain this technology to the broader community while understanding how the technology is actually being adopted. We develop education programs for the university, engage in community advocacy for the technology, advise startups, and conduct original research.

The Docklands DAO idea emerged from a research project we undertook for the Victorian government. It was an explanation of how a DAO could be used to foster social cooperation in a distinct geographic area. Our work to operationalize this idea is in the very early stages of development, so unfortunately, I cannot say much more than that.

4. *In which areas and industries do you see the most potential for DAO adoption and why?*

I think in time people will recognize DAOs to be the general-purpose organizational form for most cooperative endeavors. The technology to link like-minded people who wish to pursue some common goal or objective now exists and DAOs will be the organizational form that they adopt.

Probably, the more interesting question is: "Where won't DAOs dominate?" There the answer is in those parts of the economy that are reliant on physical capital intensity. In those parts of the economy where human capital intensity dominates, DAOs are likely to be the dominant organizational form.

5. *Where do you see the most pressing gaps in terms of DAO research to support its adoption?*

A lot of people are doing good work in developing DAO tooling. What is missing is a lot of work on governance. Many DAOs are experimenting in this space, but some hard thinking needs to be done too. At the expense of being somewhat immodest, that is what I'm trying to do.

The idea of creating "managerless" organizational forms has been around for a long time. As yet attempts to do so have been unsuccessful. One of the claims that DAO proponents make is that the advent of smart contracts will make managerless firms viable. This, however, is an empirical claim that is yet to be substantiated.

6. *Can you share your thoughts on how your work relates explicitly to the title of our book "Decentralized Autonomous Organizations: How Finance can Interact with Blockchain-based DAOs"?*

One definition of DAOs is "a community that controls a treasury." I began my academic career teaching financial economics, so I think finance has plenty to say about DAOs.

In the very instance, there are questions: How many tokens should be issued? Should there be a fixed supply or variable supply? If variable, should there be a buy-back and burn? Then should the treasury be diversified, or only hold the native token? If diversified, how much of the native token should be held for day-to-day operations (this is old-fashioned cash management)?

7. *How can academia, industry, and government work closer in the experimentation and implementation of DAOs?*

I think that academics should embed themselves into various DAOs and learn from the experience. That is what I have done — the knowledge exchange has gone in both directions. I have learned how these organizations work in practice while sharing my economic and business knowledge with the DAO members. It has also deepened my understanding of how the economy works as I have pondered new and interesting economic questions as they arise.

Governments should adopt DAO-friendly regulatory and tax policies that allow mainstreaming of this organizational form. In practice, that should be something along the lines of recognizing DAOs as being similar to partnerships but with limited liability. I'm not a lawyer, so there may be other problems with that idea, but certainly, the unrelenting hostility to DAOs and crypto is a short-sighted approach on the part of governments.

8. Let's imagine a future where DAOs are ubiquitous in the world of collaboration and business. How do you think that world compares to today?

At the moment, that world seems to be a long way away. On the other hand, change occurs quickly when it does occur, so 10 years could be a reasonable guess. Certainly, DAOs and blockchain will revolutionize the economy and society. A peer-to-peer economic system actually brings humans closer to each other and that must always be a good thing. So, the future is bright. Certainly brighter than the past. So, rather than being fearful of this new technology and organizational forms, we should be encouraging people to embrace them.

7.4　DAO perspective: Bill Laboon, Web3 Foundation/ Parity Technologies/Polkadot

1. Please introduce yourself to our readers.

My name is Bill Laboon, Director of Education and Governance Initiatives at Web3 Foundation. I've been working in various roles at Web3 Foundation helping to grow the Polkadot ecosystem since 2019. Among these are starting the Polkadot Wiki (the source of truth for Polkadot) and growing the technical education team, being the only member of the original support team for Polkadot and then growing that function into an independent team, managing our grants and community teams, and speaking to a variety of industry and academic organizations about Polkadot and the Web3 philosophy and technology.

Prior to this, I taught computer science at the University of Pittsburgh for 5 years, focusing on software engineering and quality assurance, but also teaching other courses such as "Cryptocurrency and Blockchain Technology." I am the author of two books, *A Friendly Introduction to Software Testing*, an undergraduate-level textbook, and *Strength in Numbers*, a science-fiction novel set in a world where cryptocurrency has entirely eliminated traditional money. Additionally, I have spent 15 years as a professional software engineer, working for companies such as Northrop Grumman, General Dynamics, and the UPMC Technology Development Center.

2. What is Polkadot's value proposition, and can you share some of its evolution and ambition?

The idea behind Polkadot is to provide a heterogeneously sharded blockchain environment with true interoperability and shared security. In other words, anyone can make their own blockchain using the Polkadot SDK and trustlessly communicate with other chains in the Polkadot ecosystem while sharing in the security of the entire Polkadot network. This sharding allows almost infinite experimentation with every aspect of the rules of the blockchain since the runtimes of blockchains are specified in Webassembly, which is Turing complete. It also allows for extreme efficiency and scalability, orders of magnitude better than legacy chains such as Ethereum.

3. What led to the formation of Polkadot DAO? Is it registered as a legal entity? If not, are there plans to do so?

The Polkadot "DAO" is really the Polkadot relay chain's governance mechanism. Polkadot governance enables automatic enactment of any decisions made through governance. This is because decisions are made by proposing specific "extrinsic calls" (similar to transactions on other chains), which can do anything from modifying staking parameters, issuing a remark (comment), or even changing the entire runtime (code) of the chain itself. Unlike many other DAOs, there is no need for any human intervention to actually perform what the users of the chain voted on, or any way for a human to halt the execution of something that a majority of DOT holders voted on.

The evolution of Polkadot's governance was a slow and specific process. Initially, Polkadot was launched as a proof-of-authority network, with only Web3 Foundation validators producing blocks and a sudo key owned by several key stakeholders, which could make any change to the network they desired. These were quickly removed over the next few months as the network proved stable, and "Gov1" was introduced. This allowed DOT holders to vote on referenda to change the network, but there was a "Polkadot Council" of elected accounts which could produce their own referenda which required less than a majority to pass, and a Technical Committee which could veto or modify the voting period of referenda. The current governance system, "Polkadot Opengov," is a form of direct democracy (where $1\,\mathrm{DOT} = 1\,\mathrm{vote}$) and there are no "first-class citizens," i.e. accounts with more power than others.

The Polkadot network itself, or its governance, is not currently registered as a legal entity and there are no specific plans to do so at this time.

4. What is the relationship between Parity Technologies, Web3 Foundation, and your DAO? Are there other legal entities in the family?

Web3 Foundation is a Swiss "Stiftung" (foundation), based in Zug, Switzerland, with a stated goal of "fund research and development teams who are building the foundation of the decentralized web." Web3 Foundation has approximately 50 employees, with a majority based in Switzerland. While the main focus of this funding is research and development costs directly related to Polkadot, there has been other research and funding done for other projects related to its mission, such as libp2p. Development is almost entirely done by other entities, and grants have also been given for external research. Web3 Foundation also has a large internal research team which has published papers on cryptography, game theory, distributed systems, and other topics.

Parity is a for-profit company which has been tasked with producing various software projects throughout its history. Parity initially started working on the Parity Ethereum client (which was later decentralized as "OpenEthereum") and other projects, such as the

Parity Zcash client (later rebranded as Zebra and the codebase given to the Zcash Foundation). However, as time went on, more of its focus was put into developing Polkadot and related software, including the Polkadot SDK, the ink! programming language, and Polkadot Vault. Web3 Foundation has funded Parity for the development of Polkadot.

Polkadot is itself a decentralized network and the DOT holders make all decisions in the ecosystem. While the development of Polkadot was funded by Web3 Foundation and performed mostly by Parity (although other teams such as Quadrivium and Chainsafe are building Polkadot, following the Polkadot Specification released by Web3 Foundation), these entities have no control over Polkadot itself other than by voting with their DOT.

Additionally, Web3 Foundation has funded hundreds of other projects building in the Polkadot ecosystem through its various grants programs.

5. *What are the challenges for Polkadot DAO when facing traditional financial institutions as clients, counterparties, or business partners?*

Not having a legal entity to countersign agreements can be a challenge, and I would argue the greatest one. Large institutions are hesitant to work without a traditional signatory as counterparty (and cryptographic signatures don't count for much with them).

I think the key issue here is a regulatory framework to be put into place to allow a mechanism for both of these to interact; a pathway between these two different worlds (at least until traditional companies can also be governed by DAOs). Right now, there are many gaps, or even contradictions, in blockchain law in most jurisdictions.

The development of these pathways is likely inevitable, although will take a long time — likely on the order of decades — to evolve and fully come into play. Traditional business case law is still being debated and changed on a regular basis despite corporations existing for centuries. Although I want to clarify that I am not an expert in business law, I would expect a big challenge in the upcoming years to be the contradictions less than the gaps, whereas in the near future, it will likely be the gaps that are the issues.

These contradict ions will take place between different regulatory environments (e.g. Swiss law vs. US law) as well as between different blockchains. Another challenge will be dealing with blockchains which are "decentralized in name only;" due to the fast-paced nature and pseudonymous qualities of most blockchain ecosystems, I think it will be difficult to create a universally agreed-upon definition delineating what is "sufficiently decentralized."

6. *Can you share your thoughts on how your work as a moderator of DAO Governance relates explicitly to the title of our book, Decentralized Autonomous Organizations: How Finance can Interact with Blockchain-based DAOs?*

"Moderator" is a good word for what I do in terms of governance; perhaps, a better one would be "diplomat." I don't have a lot of power myself, and Web3 Foundation tries to remain neutral on proposals that are not directly harmful to the network. This allows the community to make decisions on things, such as spending the on-chain Polkadot Treasury (which as of February 2024 holds approximately 42.7 million DOT, worth around $325 million USD at current prices). Much of what I do involves explaining the position of Web3 Foundation and educating others to empower them to make decisions with their DOT.

Some of this involves acting as a liaison between traditional companies and organizations and the Polkadot ecosystem, explaining the processes, benefits, and drawbacks to both sides.

There have been quite a few examples of Polkadot interacting with external teams through its on-chain governance, including working with the Reuters Foundation to help journalists understand blockchain, running the Polkadot Blockchain Academy to teach software engineers how to develop on Polkadot, and paying development teams directly for building tools useful to Polkadot users, such as Subwallet.

7. Let's imagine a future where DAOs are ubiquitous in the world of collaboration and business. How do you think that world compares to today?

I think the biggest benefit of blockchain technology, and this applies equally well to DAOs, is transparency and provability. When I send money from one bank to another, I have no direct proof that they are doing it, only what my banks and my banks' software tell me. When I send bitcoin or DOT from one address to another, not only can I verify this transfer in multiple ways, I can verify the entire blockchain from the genesis block to now to ensure that not only my transaction but also every transaction that was ever made is valid.

Similarly, when I send in my votes for a shareholders' meeting, I have no proof that they actually were counted. Of course, I can just trust the companies and the auditors, but we have seen many cases in the past where entities composed of humans were not trustworthy.

In my opinion, a world where DAOs are ubiquitous is a world where there is, in the words of the Web3 Foundation, "less trust, more truth." Fully audited financial statements, fully transparent and provable shareholder votes, cryptographically signed statements that cannot be retroactively edited... this is a world where economic growth is not restricted to only places where there is an expensive legal, social, and regulatory infrastructure against corruption, but to anyone, anywhere, that can afford a cheap (and becoming increasingly cheaper) computing device.

8. Are there any other thoughts you would want to share?

I have been a big believer in DAOs for a long time and Polkadot governance is the best form that I have seen for a DAO. Too many DAOs simply consist of multisigs and a smart contract for voting, which only shows votes and does not allow actual enactment without human intervention. We have seen cases of teams ignoring instructions from DAO votes or there simply being disputes in how to interpret votes. What is needed is something like Polkadot governance, where the actions which will be taken if a vote passes are provable beforehand and specified explicitly — where "code is law." As more projects migrate on-chain, and are thus accessible to DAOs, we will see this happen more often.

On the topic of "code is law," we are still early in producing true production-quality code for many DAOs and other blockchain products. Because of this, bugs and exploits are sadly quite common. It is understandable that under these circumstances, sticking too dogmatically to "code is law" is not advisable; otherwise, any hacker who discovers an exploit can be considered the rightful owner of assets controlled by a DAO, which is certainly not an acceptable outcome. While the short-term solution may be regulatory in nature, I would like to see more focus on making blockchain code developed similarly to software developed for medical devices or other life-critical systems, where major bugs are rare and worthy of inspection. This has obvious implications for the speed of development in the blockchain industry, but if we want traditional finance institutions to take us seriously, we need to develop software seriously.

Chapter 8

Conclusion and Outlook: What is Next for DAOs

Abstract

Achieving seamless interaction between financial institutions and decentralized autonomous organizations (DAOs) requires navigating complex legal, regulatory, technical, security, privacy, and educational challenges. Legal and regulatory hurdles include unclear legal recognition, ambiguous tax status, consumer protection, and securities compliance. Technical limitations involve interoperability issues and quantum computing risks. Robust security and privacy measures are crucial for fostering trust and participation. Education is essential to overcoming resistance and enabling effective engagement. The rise of a tokenized economy will put DAOs and financial institutions adapting to digital assets at an advantage. In a world where DAOs are ubiquitous, decentralized governance can create more transparent, efficient, and inclusive systems across communities, corporations, non-profits, and governments. DAOs are a form of institutional evolution and have the potential to reshape the world.

8.1 Learnings

The advent of DAOs heralds a new era of organization and collaboration. While mainstream adoption is approaching, financial institutions must prepare to interact with DAOs. As they evolve from the current experimental stage to established entities with fast-growing treasury portfolios, they will emerge as clients, service providers, and even as lucrative investment opportunities.

We developed a DAO framework and risk assessment methodology to help financial institutions navigate the unfamiliar territory of DAO ecosystems. Our DAO framework organizes DAOs across seven categories: objectives, community, governance, economics, finance, technology, and legal and regulatory. By delving into the intricacies of each category and its associated features, institutions will develop a comprehensive understanding of DAOs and know how to compare them. After categorization, subsequent interaction with DAOs is not a straightforward task. These decentralized entities pose a unique set of risks that differ significantly from those of conventional organizations that financial institutions typically deal with. To effectively address these potential pitfalls, our risk assessment methodology is designed to identify, assess, and monitor six DAO idiosyncratic areas of concern: accountability risk, community risk, financial risk, governance risk, operational risk, and technology risk. The risk assessment methodology is then applied to the case studies of MakerDAO and KlimaDAO. These real-world examples serve as simple starting guides for financial institutions to build deeper and more thorough analyses for their specific needs of DAO interaction.

To further enrich the understanding of DAOs, four distinguished experts offer their unique perspectives on the opportunities and challenges that lie at the intersection of financial services and DAOs. Their collective knowledge and experience span the legal, service provider, academic, and DAO governance domains to provide a holistic view.

8.2   Overcoming adoption challenges

The path to creating an environment in which financial institutions and DAOs can interact seamlessly is complex and demanding. To encapsulate the obstacles for further adoption, we list the following legal and regulatory hurdles, technical limitations, security and privacy, and educational challenges.

8.2.1   *Overcoming legal and regulatory hurdles*

The lack of clear and globally standardized legal recognition for DAOs poses a significant challenge to their widespread adoption and hinders interaction with traditional financial services entities. Without a well-defined legal framework, DAOs operate in a gray area, creating uncertainty about their rights, obligations, and potential liabilities. In addition, the ambiguous tax status of DAOs and their members is a potential deterrent due to potential tax liabilities and compliance burdens. The global nature of DAOs further complicates taxation issues, as members may be subject to different tax laws and regulations depending on their country of residence. Several countries and jurisdictions are making strides in passing laws and regulations to encourage the growth and legitimacy of DAOs. In the US, the states of Wyoming, Tennessee, and Vermont have been at the forefront, enacting specific legislation that recognizes DAOs as legal entities. In Switzerland, DAOs can choose to be foundations or associations.[1] The DAO Suisse association is actively working on making Switzerland the go-to place for DAOs globally by collaborating between industry and academia to advocate for clear regulations for the benefit of DAO members.

Even though consumer protection laws are not often discussed in the context of DAOs, members should know about their rights and avenues for redress. Consumer protection laws often provide mechanisms for recourse if consumers are wronged. While dispute resolution in the physical world has evolved over centuries with established legal systems, courts, and mediation processes, DAOs are still in their infancy. In the event of a breach of trust or unfair treatment within a DAO, members might have comparatively limited recourse. This challenge is addressed alongside the growing legal and regulatory acceptance of DAOs, together with the innovative use of decentralized dispute resolution methods. DAO disclosure is still limited. At the time of writing, there are no established reporting guidelines for DAO. To improve customer protection, DAOs should consider minimal disclosure requirements when issuing their tokens (Liebau and Krapels, 2021). The company

---

[1]https://www.linkedin.com/posts/dao-suisse_dao-daos-switzerland-activity-7192 048613936504832-egpq (accessed on 7 June 2024).

Bluprynt helps token issuers to be compliant with emerging disclosure requirements.[2]

As discussed throughout this book, many DAOs issue tokens as a form of financing and to incentivize participation in decision-making through governance mechanisms. Financial regulators around the world could classify governance tokens as securities. If so, DAOs will be subject to burdensome and possibly expensive regulatory requirements for registration, disclosure, and investor protection. The decentralized and borderless nature of DAOs makes it challenging to navigate the patchwork of securities regulations across different jurisdictions. To enable the positive opportunities DAOs can bring to communities, regulatory bodies must adapt existing or create new frameworks to oversee DAOs. The process of regulatory overhaul has already begun. In Singapore IRAS, the local tax authority has published a clear definition of token types. In Switzerland, entities can maintain their own capitalization table, enabling companies and DAOs to issue native digital securities (NDS) on a blockchain (Lambert *et al.*, 2021). In Liechtenstein, the government implemented a blockchain that serves as the source of truth for company-level data. In Europe, the Markets in Crypto-Assets Regulation (MiCA) allows fully decentralized DAOs to operate outside the regulation. The requirement to do so is to demonstrate that the DAO is fully decentralized.[3] In our view, it is a matter of time before other jurisdictions will take bold action to bring regulatory clarity to the world of DAOs.

Regulators may view the anonymity and lack of transparency in some DAOs as potential vectors for illicit activities, such as money laundering, terrorist financing, or sanctions evasion. This is related to what we call accountability risk in Chapter 5. Consequently, DAOs may face increased scrutiny and pressure to implement robust AML/KYC/CTF controls, which can be costly, time-consuming,

---

[2]https://www.bluprynt.com (accessed on 7 June 2024).

[3]https://cms.law/en/int/publication/legal-experts-on-markets-in-crypto-assets-mica-regulation/performing-services-in-a-decentralised-manner-under-micar (accessed on 7 June 2024).

and, importantly, antithetical to the decentralized ethos. Balancing the need for integrity with the benefits of decentralization and privacy presents a dilemma. Cryptography may be the answer to this dilemma. For example, researchers at Cornell Tech in New York have proposed CanDID (Maram *et al.*, 2020). CanDID offers a digital identity solution that solves the accountability risk while preserving privacy. It even facilitates the identification and blocking of misbehaving or criminal users. While beyond our book's scope, we highly recommend reading the entire article. Another solution by Singapore-based Hela Labs proposes a public blockchain that can interface with government-run digital identity services such as SingPass to tackle AML/KYC/CTF issues.[4] These developments encourage a more private and compliant operating model for DAOs.

8.2.2 *Technical limitations*

Interoperability is a significant challenge for DAOs. First, traditional financial services usually run on old and centralized IT systems and where they use blockchains, they presently prefer private ones. This lack of compatibility hinders the seamless transfer of assets and data, making it difficult for DAOs to interact with traditional financial services entities. A solution by the Axelar project, for example, has been used in Singapore MAS Project Guardian to exchange digital assets and currencies across different networks seamlessly.[5] Second, public blockchain networks operate using distinct protocols and standards. Axelar also tackles the DAO-to-DAO communication issues with its interoperability platform. It has built connections between blockchain ecosystems such as Ethereum and Cosmos, enabling interactions between DAOs on these platforms.

The advent of quantum computing poses a long-term challenge to the security of DAOs and the underlying blockchain infrastructure. As quantum computers become more powerful, they may be capable of breaking the cryptographic algorithms that currently secure

---

[4]https://helalabs.com/hela-whitepaper.pdf (accessed on 7 June 2024).
[5]https://www.mas.gov.sg/-/media/mas-media-library/development/fintech/guardian/interlinking-networks-technical-paper-vfinal.pdf.

blockchain networks. This potential vulnerability could undermine the integrity of DAOs, putting funds and sensitive information at risk. Cryptographers working on smart contract platforms are already developing strategies to make their protocols quantum-resistant. Examples include Algorand, which has already created a quantum-secure version of its system, and Ethereum, which has prioritized quantum resistance in its roadmap.[6]

8.2.3 *Security and privacy*

Security must be a top priority for DAOs. High-profile security breaches and significant loss of money from the actions of hackers and malicious actors mark the history of DAOs. These incidents highlight the potential vulnerabilities in DAO smart contracts, governance mechanisms, and overall infrastructure. The lack of robust security practices can erode trust in DAOs and deter potential participants from engaging with these organizations. Building on secure smart contract platforms is the first step to achieving DAO security. But it does not stop there; savvy entrepreneurs are already working on the next levels of enhancing security to counter governance/Sybil attacks, for example, the Optimal DAO.[7]

Privacy is a critical concern that DAOs cannot overlook. Without robust privacy measures, individuals and organizations will be hesitant to engage with DAOs, as the transparency and immutability of blockchain transactions reveal sensitive financial information to the public. This lack of privacy can have severe consequences, ranging from personal security risks to compromising a company's competitive advantage or a country's national security. Many jurisdictions have implemented laws to protect the interests of individuals and ensure compliance with data protection regulations, such as PDPA in Singapore and GDPR in Europe. Failure to address privacy concerns

---

[6]https://www.algorand.foundation/news/pioneering-falcon-post-quantum-techno logy-on-blockchain; https://ethereum.org/en/roadmap/future-proofing (accessed on 7 June 2024).

[7]https://www.linkedin.com/feed/update/urn:li:activity:7147723178943938560 (accessed on 7 June 2024).

effectively could hinder the adoption of DAOs and prevent them from reaching their full potential as a transformative force in the digital economy. Cryptography is, once more, the solution. Exploring how to use cryptographic primitives such as zero-knowledge proofs, homomorphic encryption, and multi-party computation will be critical in the near term. The technology is there — it just takes a better understanding to leverage it.

8.2.4 *Education*

Every new technology incurs mixed reactions, from resistance to change to eager early adoption. Blockchain-based DAOs are no different. The current interfaces for interacting with blockchain networks and participating in DAOs can be complex and intimidating for non-technical users. Navigating various wallets, understanding cryptographic concepts, and engaging with governance protocols are real deterrents for individuals and firms alike. Established institutions often have deeply entrenched legacy systems, processes, and mindsets that are difficult to disrupt. The concepts of cryptography, decentralized governance, and token-based incentives are foreign to corporate executives accustomed to hierarchical structures and centralized control. Overcoming such resistance requires a radical shift in perspective and a willingness to adapt. Investing in education about blockchain and DAOs to learn about their benefits and risks will help individuals and communities interact with DAOs in discerning ways. At the same time, DAO and blockchain industry builders are constantly improving their products to make them more user-friendly. The combination of education and better user experience (UX) will undoubtedly help increase DAO participation.

8.3 Conclusion

In this section of our closing chapter, we outline a possible future where blockchain-based DAOs are adopted globally and across industries. We examine two areas: the tokenized economy and the decentralized governance to help financial services professionals seize the opportunities that DAO adoption may present to them.

8.3.1 *Tokenized economy*

This subsection describes the impact of tokenization on assets, decentralized finance (DeFi) markets, automated and cross-border payments, financial inclusion, and automated taxation.

Tokenization is the process of converting physical world assets, such as property, art, or commodities, into digital tokens on a blockchain network. This process enables fractional ownership, allowing investors to purchase a portion of an asset that would otherwise be too expensive to acquire individually. Tokenization streamlines the transfer of ownership, reduces transaction costs, and increases transparency, as all transactions are recorded on the immutable blockchain ledger. Tokenized assets are digital assets. Digital assets will change the financial landscape by providing new avenues for investment, value transfer, and asset ownership. They will also assist in making the current financial system more efficient. Augustin Karstens, General Manager of the Bank of International Settlements, and his co-author Nandan Nilekani describe their vision of a new financial ecosystem that uses tokenization and distributed ledger (or blockchain) technology, as the Finternet (Karstens and Nilekani, 2024).[8] As crypto-native organizations, DAOs manage digital assets seamlessly, which puts them at an advantage. Traditional financial services institutions will need to "migrate" to the Finternet. If you are part of a financial institution that wants to interact, partner, and serve DAOs in the future of the tokenized economy, having read our book will give you an essential edge.

DeFi markets are an emerging force in financial services. In a recent episode of the Blockchain Scholars Podcast, Professor Dr. Andreas Park of the Rotman School of Management at Toronto University in Canada described in his recent work investigating the use of automated market makers (AMM), a DeFi primitive that allows buyers and sellers of tokens to swap their holdings

---

[8]On a sidenote, we find it remarkable that even the head of the Bank of International Settlements now speaks about using distributed ledger technology and cryptographic primitives to re-design the global financial ecosystem.

without an intermediary, as "Science Fiction."[9] By eliminating intermediaries and automating processes through smart contracts, DeFi markets offer greater transparency, security, and accessibility compared to conventional financial markets. In their working paper, Park and his coauthor Malinova (2024) estimate that the US equity markets could save billions in transaction fees by using AMMs. As more and more assets get tokenized, DeFi primitives become an attractive and global marketplace, drawing in DAOs, financial services firms, and individuals.

In the tokenized economy, smart contracts enable DAOs to automate complex financial transactions, such as multi-step payments or escrow services. This technology enables DAOs to automate global payments to their contractors, suppliers, or partners in different countries. With such automated payment systems, DAOs can reduce transaction costs, increase transparency, and ensure timely and secure payments with fewer intermediaries. How does a financial institution become one of the few intermediaries then? For now, there is a regulatory moat, for example, crypto on- and off-ramps require a license. In Singapore, the Monetary Authority has created the Payment Services Act that covers digital token services. But once the tokenized economy is a reality, market participants will require less and less interaction with the fiat world. DAOs and other digitally savvy firms will settle their transactions natively on blockchain platforms. Regulators will develop suitable frameworks to oversee this type of activity. Only financial services firms that keep up with these developments will remain relevant.

The tokenized economy will also have a significant impact on financial inclusion: New business models will evolve. For example, the Algorand platform has extremely low requirements for running a validating node as part of its blockchain protocol network. At the time of our writing, a Raspberry Pi 5 computer with 8 GB of RAM is available for less than USD 100. In communities that are excluded from traditional finance today, these small computers could

---

[9] https://youtube.com/playlist?list=PLyy_BMKWX3SQfgJ3VhHv7hTbc28lJjl3 G&si=Ml7pInYFZQTgX5KA (accessed on 7 June 2024).

be bought and used to generate fee income in cryptocurrency from blockchain validation. The proceeds could then be used as collateral for loans on DeFi platforms to purchase everyday items or make small investments. Small communities could even organize themselves as DAOs to decide which hardware to buy and which blockchain to validate and to make other decisions jointly.

Automated taxation is a topic that is challenging today but will be important in the fully tokenized economy where even tax regulation resides as a rule in a smart contract. DAOs could automatically calculate and allocate tax liabilities based on predefined rules, ensuring accuracy and transparency. This automation could reduce the administrative burden on DAOs and other firms, allowing them to focus on their core objectives while maintaining compliance with relevant tax regulations. Enabling real-time tax calculations and payments based on the specific rules and rates of the respective jurisdiction may also allow DAOs to manage their treasury portfolio more efficiently. However, the benefits expand beyond DAOs and digitally savvy firms. Governments could explore collecting taxes directly from transactions recorded on blockchains. This could lead to a more efficient and transparent tax system, reducing the likelihood of tax evasion and ensuring a more equitable distribution of resources for all citizens, including DAO members.

8.3.2 *A future with DAOs*

Historically, many DAOs have been associated with the negative elements of the crypto community where extreme greed is rife. For DAOs to be relevant and legitimate in the future, we envision communities that use DAOs to achieve their common goals beyond speculating in tokens.

In a world where DAOs are widely adopted, communities, corporations, non-profits, and even governments can use the power of decentralized governance to create more transparent, efficient, and inclusive systems. Communities could use DAOs to facilitate decision-making and resource allocation, ensuring that the needs and desires of all members are heard and addressed. Imagine a local community using a DAO to manage a shared green space, with members proposing and voting on projects and funds being automatically dispensed based on the outcomes. This democratic, self-governing approach could lead to stronger, more resilient communities. Corporations could adopt DAOs to foster greater stakeholder engagement and align incentives. Employees, customers, and suppliers could have a direct say in company decisions, with their contributions and participation rewarded through token-based incentives. This could lead to more agile, responsive organizations that better serve the needs of all stakeholders. For example, during the research for this book, we spoke to a chief digital and information officer of a leading life insurance company with a large agent force. On an exploratory basis, the leader asked our opinion about using the DAO concept for agents to collaborate and make decisions. Non-profits could use DAOs to increase transparency and accountability in their operations, with donors and beneficiaries having a clear view of how their funds are used and what results are achieved. Governments could experiment with DAOs to increase citizen engagement and trust. For example, a city could use a DAO to gather citizen input and allow them to propose, vote, and make decisions on budget allocation directly. This would be an antidote to the recent growing reach of authoritarianism and lead to more responsive and accountable governments. Some tech entrepreneurs have gone as far as to recommend "network states" built on decentralized digital networks to replace nation states and physical geographical boundaries.[10] Although we rate the desirability and possibility of such networked states as low for now, there are still many other promising principles underlying DAOs explored by other future-focused thinkers. In *Radical Markets: Uprooting Capitalism and Democracy for a Just Society*, Posner and Weyl (2018) present a series of inventive ideas, including quadratic voting (QV), to restructure economic and social systems to create more equitable and efficient outcomes. Since then, QV has been tested in small

---

[10]https://thenetworkstate.com/ (accessed on 7 June 2024).

ways in the physical world and used in some prominent DAOs.[11,12] "Programmable politics," a concept introduced by Muthukrishna (2023) in *A Theory of Everyone*, envisions human cooperation and innovation being enhanced through technology. DAOs embody this vision by creating programmable governance structures that can adapt and evolve in real time, promoting transparency, accountability, and inclusivity. In this future world, DAOs will simply be another form of organization and ubiquitous. They would be as familiar and easy to use as any other digital platform. User-friendly interfaces, clear educational resources, and robust dispute resolution mechanisms would make participating in DAOs accessible to everyone. These visionary concepts are an indication of DAOs' promise in how we can organize, govern, and innovate at both local and global scales to reshape our world. As the finance industry learns to interact with DAOs, we stand on the cusp of a new era of financial innovation and value creation.

References

Karstens, A. and Nilekani, N., 2024. Finternet: The Financial System for the Future. *BIS Working Paper*. https://www.bis.org/publ/work1178.htm.

Lambert, T., Liebau, D., and Roosenboom, P., 2021. Security Token Offerings. *Small Business Economics*. https://link.springer.com/article/10.1007/s11187-021-00539-9.

Liebau, D. and Krapels, N., 2021. An Exploratory Essay on Minimum Disclosure Requirements for Cryptocurrency and Utility Token Issuers. *Cryptoeconomic Systems*. https://cryptoeconomicsystems.pubpub.org/pub/liebau-minimum-disclosure/release/11.

Maram, D., Malvai, H., Zhang, F., Nerla, J.L., Frolov, A., Kell, T., Lobban, T., Moy, C., Juels, A., and Miller, A., 2020. CanDID: Can-Do Decentralized Identity with Legacy Compatibility, Sybil-Resistance, and Accountability. *Working Paper*. https://www.arijuels.com/wpcontent/uploads/2020/07/Candid.pdf.

Muthukrishna, M., 2023. *A Theory of Everyone: The Signs of Who We Are, How We Got Here and Where We're Going*. https://mitpress.mit.edu/9780262048378/a-theory-of-everyone.

---

[11] https://www.radicalxchange.org/wiki/colorado-qv/ (accessed on 7 June 2024).
[12] https://www.radicalxchange.org/wiki/nyc-qv/ (accessed on 7 June 2024).

Park, A. and Malinova, K., 2024. Learning from DeFi: Would Automated Market Makers Improve Equity Trading? *Working Paper.* https://papers.ssrn.com/sol3/papers.cfm?abstract_id=4531670.

Posner, E. and Weyl, G., 2018. *Radical Markets: Uprooting Capitalism and Democracy for a Just Society.* https://press.princeton.edu/books/hardcover/9780691177502/radical-markets.

Afterword

1 Introduction

After more than a decade of experimentation, since Satoshi created bitcoin, blockchain is finally impacting our lives and reshaping multiple industries. My name is Sunny Lu, and I am the Founder of vechain, a smart contract blockchain platform launched in 2017. I have witnessed these developments first-hand as an entrepreneur and community builder, for example, in the context of counterfeit luxury goods and the development of sustainability initiatives. I believe blockchain's transformation potential for societies will rival the internet's. One of blockchain's revolutionary ideas is to challenge the traditional setup of companies and replace it with organizations founded for social collaboration. Decentralized autonomous organizations (DAOs) are one of such results. DAOs operate transparently, are controlled by the organizations' members, and are not dominated or heavily influenced by any centralized entity or individual, including the world's governments.

2 History

Over the last few centuries of entrepreneurial venture development, there have always been three distinct critical contributors: the innovators with intellectual property and the ability to develop their knowledge into a product, the investors who provide capital to the enterprise, and the employees or workforce, who assist the entrepreneur in building the venture. This division of responsibilities helps maximize efficiency and productivity while focusing all parties toward a single mission. Today, companies structured in this way account for most enterprises worldwide. Companies should be dynamic and agile to evolve swiftly to overcome the challenges of a volatile world. However, recent events (e.g. COVID's impact on supply chains) have shown that the expected dynamism and agility at the global level are often missing, and there are several "bottlenecks" or issues with the existing model. Some of these issues include increased complexity, organizational and operational risks, supply chain vulnerabilities, environmental and social responsibilities, and innovation challenges, to name a few. Additionally, if a company lacks transparency and robust governance processes, it is more susceptible to corruption.

3   A solution

DAOs, as a new form of organization, provide a solution for these issues. Their democratic decision-making process promotes a more equitable relationship among members. It empowers individuals to create innovations and run efficient operations without the constraints of the typical corporate structure. While there are still many legal, technical, and design challenges, I am confident that in the near future, DAOs will play a much more critical role than they do today. Once the adoption spreads more widely across industries, it will drive the evolution of the DAO concept, increasing its economic importance even further. In particular, the governance models of DAOs will develop far beyond the current simplistic majority voting systems. I expect more equitable governance frameworks to be designed and delivered along with technology development. There will also be improvements in reputation systems, delegated voting with categorized expertise, liquid democracy, identity systems with privacy protection, and dispute resolution systems. This will support scalable decision-making processes for a wide variety of business scenarios. Other than the current DAO experiments in decentralized finance, venture capital, and crowdfunding, other areas are currently emerging, for example, sustainability.

3.1 *Supply chain and sustainability*

I believe that DAOs will greatly benefit supply chain management and sustainability-related activities. Growing geopolitical tensions and nationalistic tendencies have pressured businesses and non-profit groups to find more innovative ways to collaborate globally. In supply chain management, we must deal with challenges from transportation and logistics constraints, supply and demand imbalances, cybersecurity threats, regulatory compliance, environmental matters, and labor shortages. Tomorrow's global supply chain requires transparency, traceability, cost-efficiency, low lead times, and broad geographic coverage. Let us imagine a future with DAOs: Suppliers and purchasers along a supply chain start a DAO whose mission overlaps theirs. In this situation, their objectives could be beyond profit.

For example, their objectives could be to improve sustainability metrics jointly. Implementing DAOs in this fashion will ensure that all parties involved in the supply chain have a say in allocating resources efficiently while meeting individual obligations. A DAO's transparency will also help reduce fraud.

Climate change is one of the most pressing challenges of our times. As such, it is of utmost urgency for governments, businesses, and individuals to change our behaviors and practices with sustainability and circularity as goals. The biggest challenge in sustainability development is building effective co-working relationships among stakeholders. Here, DAOs offer an innovative and inclusive way of organizing and coordinating. DAOs can be set up to pursue universal goals with sustainability frameworks to attract like-minded members. By leveraging decentralized and transparent decision-making processes, DAOs can be used in renewable energy initiatives and community-based environmental programs. DAOs foster inclusive adoption and enable community members to have their voices heard in projects that affect them. This helps align initiatives with local needs and values.

Sustainability should be everyone's responsibility, and good behavior should be rewarded. Decentralized solutions using blockchain technology can deliver incentives to individuals based on their efforts. In November 2023, vechain and AWorld organized an experiment on sustainability challenges in Turin, Italy. In just a few weeks, 2,400 participants logged 450,000 small actions from their daily lives, saving 3 million CO_2 (more than 1,000 long-haul flights) and 9 million gallons of water (equal to 14 Olympic-sized swimming pools). We organized this experiment to trial some of the activities we plan to support with our own DAO. After decades of development of corporate social responsibility and regulations in climate change driven by corporations, I foresee this type of collective effort will have more significant business value and that it can collectively be monetized using DAOs. They can organize challenges involving people worldwide to create value and ensure the proper and fair distribution of benefits.

DAOs can offer new ways to fund and invest in sustainable development projects, mobilizing resources from a broad base of investors and stakeholders interested in supporting sustainable initiatives. DAOs can facilitate global partnerships by connecting individuals and organizations across borders to work on sustainability initiatives despite the limitations of time zones, geographical locations, jurisdictions, languages, and cultural differences. These international collaborations can accelerate the exchange of ideas, resources, and best practices for sustainability developments.

While DAOs offer promising avenues for advancing sustainability, they also could face challenges such as regulatory recognition, security issues, frauds, manipulations, and judicial executions. As the technology and regulatory framework evolve, DAO will become an increasingly critical infrastructure in pursuing sustainability development and implementations globally.

3.2   *VeBetterDAO*

vechain launched VeBetterDAO (vebetterdao.org) to explore DAO implementation for sustainability. With our clear objective, profound design, consent governance model, and proper technical deliveries, a DAO is the correct organizational form to empower people, boost innovation, and improve productivity and efficiency by maximizing the utility and value of small teams. In VeBetterDAO, this happens through seamless collaboration use cases. It excels with community-driven projects with high participation, open-sourced developments relying on innovations from sharing and exchange, transparent and equitable operations with aligned interests, highly adaptable initiatives, etc.

4 The future

The future of DAOs will involve integrative developments with other technologies like the Internet of Things (IoT) and artificial intelligence (AI). Such developments could enhance automation, decentralization, and data integrity with fewer human interventions and create the possibility of DAO adoption in previously unattainable ways. DAOs could govern smart cities, including managing traffic control systems and energy distributions with limited human operations. DAOs can make autonomous decisions about resource allocation, infrastructure improvements, and emergency responses based on data collected from billions of IoT devices without centralized control. Other areas where DAOs could add value include environmental monitoring, autonomous transportation, and decentralized property management. AI can enhance the decision-making processes within a DAO by providing data-driven insights, predictive analytics, simulations, and modeling. This will give community members more options to make more scientific assessments and judgments. We could also use AI to support evaluations of collected data.

A great example is the use of AI to analyze a photograph or file uploaded by users to justify and quantify the sustainable actions in a DAO ecosystem. The receipts of electric vehicle (EV) supercharge sessions can be analyzed for the type of electricity used, the energy utilized, and the mileage traveled, leading to an autonomous decision to incentivize the user within the DAO ecosystem. Through the synchronized developments in IoT, AI, and blockchains, DAOs can manage digital assets and operations and support the off-chain world. The seamless integration with the physical world could allow operational decisions to be made based on real-time data and collective governance. Also, DAOs will become more interoperable across different blockchain platforms, facilitating cross-chain collaborations, asset management, and resource allocations. These advances will enable DAOs to leverage the strengths of various blockchain networks, expand their operational capabilities, and involve inclusive users' participation to support a broader scale of projects and initiatives.

In summary, despite significant challenges, the potential for DAOs in the next decade is vast and varied. It promises a future where decentralized governance models could significantly impact how we organize, collaborate, and make decisions on both small and large scales.

Sunny Lu
Founder, vechain and VeBetterDAO

Appendix A

A More Detailed Definition of What a Blockchain Is (Using Bitcoin as an Example)

Here, we present a more in-depth discussion of the different parts of Bashir's (2018) definition of a blockchain. Peer-to-peer feature suggests that no intermediaries are required for two individuals to transact. But why do we have intermediaries in today's business world at all? There are several reasons, but let's illustrate one case with an example: Say you buy shares in a startup. You have agreed on a valuation (you will buy 10% of his company for USD 10,000) with the entrepreneur. Then the question arises: Will you wire the entrepreneur the USD 10,000 first, or will he update the government ownership records first? Chances are neither of you are incentivized to go first. What if you wire the money, and the entrepreneur decides not to update the share register? What if he updates the share register that makes you the rightful owner in his company, and you choose not to wire the money? So, what is the common practice in this kind of situation apart from having a share purchase agreement? You hire an intermediary, an escrow agent. The escrow agent is neutral. You deposit the funds with them, and only when you have proof that the share register is updated will the escrow agent wire the funds to the entrepreneur. Of course, the escrow agent charges a fee for their work. The peer-to-peer feature of blockchain suggests that such escrow agent services would no longer be required since we can trust in the cryptographic mechanics of the system rather than in intermediaries.

When we talk about networks, we mean nodes or participants in a system connected through communication channels or links. There are three basic network topologies. The first is described as centralized (Baran, 1964). A single node in the center of the network connects all other nodes. A centralized system is extremely fast because of the small number of hops a piece of information must travel from the sending to the receiving node. At the same time, this topology is very error-prone. When the central node has a technical failure, then all other nodes are not able to communicate with each other. In a distributed network, nodes are connected to hubs, which have links to other hub nodes. If a hub node fails, the nodes connected to it might not be able to communicate with the rest of the network anymore. However, all other hub nodes and nodes connected to them can still operate. This system is therefore more resilient than a centralized one but also slower when propagating new information across the network. Finally, a decentralized network is one where all nodes are connected to multiple other nodes. Information can flow even if numerous nodes on the network fail; there is always an alternative route to other nodes. A decentralized system is the most resilient type of network. It is also the slowest in terms of the number of hops data has to travel from node to node.

Public key cryptography or asymmetric cryptography is one of the fundamental elements of a blockchain. It uses a pair of keys: one public and one private. While the public key can be distributed widely, the private key, as the name suggests, must be kept secret by the owner. The easiest way to think of the concepts of a public and a private key is to compare them to a bank account number and a password to authorize transactions. With only the public key, I might be able to see the balance of a wallet or account. However, I need the private key to sign the transaction if I want to transact.

Talking about the cryptographically secure feature of a blockchain would not be complete without mentioning hashing. Hashing is the passing of a dataset through an algorithm to always produce a fixed-length output. Hashes are fingerprints of datasets. Each dataset, whether "Hi" or the entire Library of Congress, has precisely one unique hash. As such, they are always deterministic, irreversible, and collision-resistant. The latter means that no two inputs can ever be the same. A prominent hashing algorithm used in the context of blockchains is called SHA-256. We will return to the importance of hashes when we discuss the next feature of the blockchain — immutability and append-only.

To explain immutability and append-only, we introduce another concept in cryptography: The Merkle Tree (Merkle, 1979). In computer science, a tree is a hierarchical tree-like structure with a root, parent, leaf, and child nodes. Instead of raw data, we can store hashes in the different nodes of a Merkle Tree (Fig. A.1). Each leaf node consists of a cryptographic hash of its original data. Every parent node is a hash of the combination of its child node's hashes. Using the Merkle root and applying the properties of cryptographic hash functions, we can tell if transactions in a block have been changed. We can also identify the specific transaction that has been amended. If a single transaction in a confirmed block is altered, the Merkle root

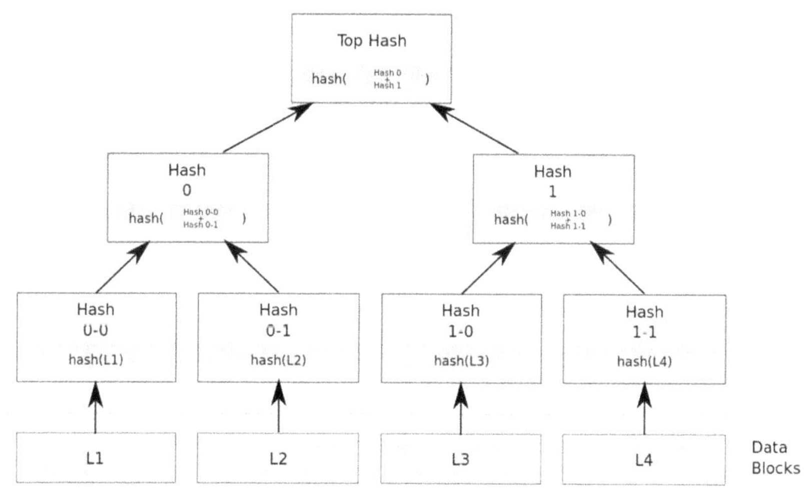

Fig. A.1. The Merkle Tree.
Source: Wikipedia.

will differ from the "correct" Merkle root. The tampering would be visible immediately. Merkle Trees also allow users to verify that their transaction has been included in a block without downloading the entire blockchain. Processes such as Simplified Payment Verification can traverse branches in the Merkle Tree and check whether a particular transaction is hashed into that tree. This efficiency level for blockchain technology would be impossible without including a Merkle root in each block.

So far, we have not explained why a blockchain is called a blockchain. If we think of a block as a notebook that contains time-stamped transactions, we can easily imagine that a blockchain is many such notebooks that are somehow connected. But how would they be connected, and why do we say a blockchain is append-only and immutable? We can assign a hash to each block. Next, we store in each newly appended block the previous block's hash. Through this process of connecting the blocks, a blockchain is created. As with Merkle Trees, we only need to look at the last block's hash in the chain to see if someone has altered this copy of the distributed ledger. This means that data stored on a blockchain is sequential. A timestamp is attached to each transaction and block (Haber and Stornetta, 1991). We cannot amend older blocks after they are recorded — the definition of immutability. You can only add new data to the ledger as part of a novel block that gets added to the chain; therefore, we say one of the properties of a blockchain is "append-only."

You may have come across the term "mining" in the context of blockchains before. Let's move on to the last feature of our blockchain definition: the consensus mechanism required to reach an agreement among peers. Now, we have quite a vocabulary in the field of blockchain. We can discuss a central issue in distributed ledgers: the consensus algorithm. We learned before that many copies of the ledger are spread across the network of nodes. To establish whether a new piece of data/a new block should be added to the blockchain, consensus needs to be established. When Nakamoto (2008) prepared their paper, they were inspired by gold miners. They thought about creating new coins and the work that must be done in return. They felt the most suitable way to do this was to compete for solving complex cryptographic riddles to validate a new block. These cryptographic riddles make use of concepts we have already learned about. For example, hashing and identifying a pseudo-random number called a nonce. Cryptographic riddles are hard to solve but easy to verify for other miners. Please remember that a consensus algorithm is a mechanism to achieve agreement about appending a new block to the blockchain. We can trust the consensus algorithm since the parties involved in verifying the transaction between you and another individual, because its rules are transparent to all and its code cannot be changed *ad-hoc*. Among all consensus algorithms, Proof of Work, Proof of Stake, Delegated Proof of Stake, and PBFT or Practical Byzantine Fault Tolerance are prominent.

References

Baran, P., 1964. On Distributed Communications Networks. *IEEE Transactions on Communications Systems.* https://doi.org/10.7249/P2626.

Bashir, I., 2018. Mastering Blockchain — Second Edition: Distributed ledger technology, decentralization, and smart contracts explained. *Packt Textbook.* https://amzn.asia/d/564eKZx.

Haber, S. and Stornetta, W.S., 1991. How to Time-Stamp a Digital Document. *J. Cryptology.* https://doi.org/10.1007/BF00196791.

Merkle R., 1979. Secrecy, Authentication, and Public Key Systems. *Electrical Engineering, PhD Thesis.* http://www.ralphmerkle.com/papers/Thesis 1979.pdf.

Nakamoto, S., 2008. Bitcoin: A Peer-to-Peer Electronic Cash System. *Working Paper.* https://bitcoin.org/bitcoin.pdf.

Index